The DRIED FLOWER *Arranger's Year*

Spring

Summer

Fall

Winter

The DRIED FLOWER Arranger's Year

A complete guide to picking, drying and arranging flowers season by season

JENNY RAWORTH & SUSAN BERRY

Photography by Mike Newton

BCA

LONDON NEW YORK SYDNEY TORONTO

DEDICATION

This book is for Ricky
and for our daughters Sophie and Kate

CONCEIVED, EDITED AND DESIGNED BY
COLLINS & BROWN LIMITED
EDITOR *Sarah Hoggett*
ART DIRECTOR *Roger Bristow*
DESIGNED BY *Carol McCleeve*

Filmset by August Filmsetting
Reproduction by Daylight, Singapore
Printed and bound in Spain by Graficromo

Contents

Spring

Summer

Autumn

Winter

Introduction

Dried flower arrangements are much simpler to make than they look, provided
you follow a few basic guidelines on colour, texture, and shape.

LOWERS, DRIED OR FRESH, make all the difference to the way a house looks and feels. An
attractive flower arrangement, even a very
simple one, immediately transforms a room,
adding life, warmth, colour, and atmosphere.

Dried flowers are particularly useful because there is a
wide choice all year round. Some flowers keep their
colour much better than others when dried, but it is easy
to refresh an arrangement once it starts to fade.

I am certainly not a lover of all forms of dried flowers
and over the years I have developed strong likes and
dislikes. There are certain kinds that you will not find in
this book, for the simple reason that I do not find them
attractive and therefore do not use them in my own
arrangements. I am not really keen on some of the more
exotic, oddly shaped flowers, unless used sparingly as a
contrast to something much softer. I am not a purist
about dried flowers and sometimes use dyed flowers.
These are fine if you take great care about the way the
arrangement is put together and make sure that the
colour and the texture harmonize. I also use silk flowers
occasionally. Provided they have a matt finish, they blend
well in most arrangements.

I also have quite strong views about how the flowers
themselves should be combined (see Blocking colours,
overleaf) and on the colour palette used. The first step in
making a good arrangement is consciously to decide to
limit the number of colours. If you restrict the colours to,
say, fewer than half a dozen, your arrangement will
immediately gain a unity that helps to offset any errors
you may have made in the shape.

First steps in dried flower arranging

Making good dried flower arrangements is an art, but
you can quickly achieve very good results if you set yourself sensible targets at the outset. My own recipe for
success for any novice flower arranger is to start by
choosing a relatively simple shape. An arrangement gains
much of its impact from its form – like the little Lavender
Pots on page 69.

The second most important element is not to rush the
arrangement. Take your time and make sure that everything is properly secured. Although you do not see it, the
base of the arrangement is crucial. If you have not made it
firm and solid, it is almost impossible to achieve a professional result. So whether it is a wreath, a garland, or a
basket of flowers, make sure that it is strong enough for
you to attach decorations to it without it coming apart. In
the projects with a tall stem like the Christmas Tree
(page 114) and the Topiary Rose Trees (page 48), a firm
base is essential to prevent the arrangement from top-
pling over. To achieve this, I bed the stems into plaster of
Paris, which sets rock hard. For wreaths and swags, you
need a good firm base to hold the decorations – either
moss or hay bound securely with wire. For most of the
arrangements set into containers, florist's dry oasis is
used, wedged tightly into the container. It should be deep
enough to anchor the flowers properly.

My last tip is to collect together all the materials you
are going to need before you start. Make a proper work
space where you do not have to clear everything away if
you do not complete the project that day, and keep the
ingredients neatly in boxes until required. If you are sys-
tematic in the way you work, you will achieve more professional results. Each project in this book lists the
equipment and flowers you need in the order that you use
them, so it is easy for you to organize the materials properly before you start. The techniques involved in creating
dried flower arrangements are not difficult to master, but
you will achieve better results if you work in an orderly,
calm atmosphere. Unless you go about it methodically, it
is all too easy to lose the flower heads in a welter of
discarded stalks and wires.

Seasonal bias

Finally, I have given the arrangements in this book a
seasonal basis, because I think it helps to understand the
nature of the ingredients you are working with. If you
buy your dried flowers from a supplier, it may not make
very much difference to you; but if you have a garden and
want to dry at least some of the ingredients yourself, you
may find it reminds you to go out and pick the flowers. I
like the fact that my dried flowers allow me to continue to
enjoy the garden after the growing season is over, even if
it is only a few bunches of home-dried lavender in an
arrangement that is otherwise bought from a supplier.

The arrangement, left, epitomizes the way I like to combine dried flowers. I often use colours with
a similar tone – the pink larkspur, the dark red amaranthus, and the pink-tinged 'Gerdo' roses
– to give the design a sense of unity.

Using colour

One of the nicest things about dried flowers is that the colours soften slightly as the flowers dry. The resulting shades of many dried flowers are extremely attractive, as the colours take on the quality of an antique tapestry. They also blend extremely well with the decoration in many rooms, so that you do not tire of the arrangement, as perhaps you would if the colours were bolder and more eye-catching. However, don't put your dried flower arrangements on a windowsill or in direct sunlight, as they will immediately start to fade.

In order to decide which colours to use in an arrangement, you need first to ask yourself a few very important questions. Where are you planning to put the arrangement? What colours will work best with the decoration of the room? Do you have china on a dresser that you wish the arrangement to complement? Will the colours work with the shape and size of arrangement you have in mind?

Some of the most effective arrangements are those in which only one colour is employed, as in the Lavender Pots on page 69, the Larkspur Bowl on page 51, or the Wheatsheaf on page 78. These are all quite architectural-looking arrangements, and the use of a single colour adds drama and emphasizes the shape.

Blocking colours

One of my key principles is to block colours together rather than dot them about. As you look at the arrangements in this book, you will see that they rely very much on the impact of densely packed flower heads making a strong colour statement. I find this has two advantages. Dried flowers, by virtue of being dried, are quite small and inevitably lose some colour in the drying process. Blocking colours helps to strengthen the colour and counteract any drabness.

Where I have put several colours together, as in the Decorated Basket on page 91, I am careful to use colours with the same degree of brightness or vibrancy. If you use one very bright colour – such as red – with other darker toned colours, you will find that the red jumps out at you and dominates the other elements in the arrangement. The colour wheel opposite, made out of flowers, shows the contrasts and progressions in the colour spectrum traditionally used by artists.

The effects of colour

There are entire books devoted to the theory and science of colour, and also to its psychological effects. Some colours – reds, pinks, yellows, and oranges – are naturally warm; others – blues, mauves, blue-greens – are naturally cool. Contrasts of colour – red and green, for example – are much more strident than colours next to each other on the colour wheel. You should consider these relationships when planning your arrangements.

Made up of different dried flowers, this colour wheel shows the progression of colours in the spectrum. Colours opposite each other contrast, while those next to each other have a similar feel. When you block colours by putting lots of dried flower heads together, the impact is far stronger than if you had scattered the flowers about.

You will also notice that colours affect each other when juxtaposed. Blue next to white gives a very different effect from blue next to green, for example. The blue becomes stronger in the first instance, more muted in the second.

White added to an arrangement has the effect of "lifting" the arrangement and breaking up the shape slightly. It draws your eye away from the overall shape. If you want to refresh an arrangement, adding white and green gives it an almost instantaneous boost.

Try to forget any rules you may have been told about certain colours not going together. Some of the best effects are achieved by using unusual combinations.

The little posies show the different effects you get from using neighbouring and contrasting colours. Colours with the same degree of brightness or vibrancy – such as blue and green in the lavender and hydrangea combination, and blue and pink in the lavender and larkspur – soften each other. Contrasting colours – such as blue and yellow in the lavender and golden rod, and blue and red in the lavender and roses – emphasize each other.

Texture and form

To make a satisfactory arrangement you need to think about the texture and shape as well as the colour. Texture is extremely important, because it prevents the arrangement from becoming too formless; the contrast provided by hard surfaces – such as pots, baskets, seed pods, nuts, and twigs – helps to emphasize the delicacy of the flowers. Creating the right balance between softness and hardness or between shiny and matt surfaces is an important element in adding interest to the arrangement.

The form the arrangement takes is also a crucial part of the whole design concept, and marrying colour and texture to form is the secret of any successful dried flower arrangement. Just as it helps to block colour together, it also helps to create blocks of shape within the arrangement and, more particularly, to contrast these. For example, hard bundles of poppy heads juxtapose wonderfully with floppy faded peony heads.

Among the decorative plants that I use to add interesting texture to arrangements are bundles of birch twigs, twigs covered in lichen, cinnamon sticks and various grasses. They are most successful if you bind them into small bundles, about 5 in (12.5 cm) long, tied with natural raffia. Nuts – chestnuts, hazelnuts (usually strung in bracelet form), and walnuts – make attractive round shapes, and can be varnished to give them an extra gloss.

Right: In these small groups, various materials have been grouped together to demonstrate how to contrast forms and textures.

The wheel, below, shows a selection of the textural elements I use in my arrangements. Generally in fairly low-key colours, they contribute to the arrangement through their texture and form, whether rough or smooth, spiky or round, matt or glossy.

Right: beiges and olive greens give the group unity of colour. The brush-like heads of wheat, the hard seed heads of poppies, the stiff shapes of the birch twigs, and the soft texture of the moss provide gentle contrasts of shape and texture.

Above: the round, hard shape of the pomegranate head is echoed in the peppercorns and set off by the soft and spiky forms of the club moss, while the bundle of coloured pasta echoes the colour of the pomegranate head.

Left: smooth and tidy pasta bows contrast with the rough, gnarled twigs covered with lichen moss, and the papery white globe of garlic sets off the rough texture of the lichen moss.

Above: the dramatic shape of the Sterculia pod is contrasted by the soft spires of the Setaria, and the neat, shiny hazelnuts.

Left; the outline of the hard clay pots is softened with Verticordia niténs spilling out of the top, while shiny orange slices contrast with the round peppercorns and walnut.

Many plants have interestingly shaped seed heads – several of the onion family have attractive globular heads, particularly the giant allium (*Allium christophii*). Poppies (*Papaver rhoeas*), love-in-a-mist (*Nigella damascena*), honesty (*Lunaria annua*), and flowers like the lotus flower also have attractive seed heads, as do some of the iris family, which split open their pods to reveal rows of seeds.

Cones also make an interesting textural contrast, as do various fruits – kumquats, oranges, and tangerines, sometimes cut in slices and varnished (see page 122).

Don't be afraid to experiment with unusual kinds of decoration. I spend a lot of time looking around for objects that have an interesting form, texture, or shape. The kitchen is a rich storehouse of ideas, and I use anything that takes my fancy, from pasta to garlic, from flower pots to biscuits. Wooden spoons, miniature loaves of bread, even pastry cutters can be put to use.

If you do use perishable produce in an arrangement, bake it or varnish it to prevent it from rotting, unless the arrangement is only intended to last for a short while.

Proportion and shape

Getting the proportions right is another key factor in the overall design. In flower arranging, you are sometimes told that the container should be one-third of the height of the whole arrangement. Frankly I do not think these so-called rules are much help. You have to learn to use your eye to make sure that the balance is correct. This means concentrating on the overall image rather than focusing on any one element within it. It may help to half-close your eyes, so that you cannot see the detail as clearly, and concentrate on the overall outline.

Dried flower arrangements can take many shapes, from simple bunches to complex wreaths and swags. An essential element in any arrangement is a firm and stable base for the flowers. A wobbly, insecure base is irritating and likely to produce an unprofessional result.

When creating an arrangement that is to go on a wall, it is much easier to get the shape right if you work on it hanging up. As you add to it, you can visualize the finished effect on the wall. Sometimes I work on the arrangement flat, but hang it at intervals to see how it is developing. I can then decide how to position the next element of the decoration for the best effect. Most arrangements need some adjustment once they are in position to achieve the right balance in the shape.

Bought dried flowers are quite expensive, and so it is worth planning the size of a project carefully before you rush off to buy the flowers. Arrangements never look good if the ingredients are sparse, so if you are making a Christmas wreath, for example, buy a small base ring, and make sure it is fully covered by the decorations, rather than opting for a larger one on which the decorations are scattered thinly.

Containers
Choosing a container for the arrangement is as important as deciding which flowers to use. Make sure that it sets off the arrangement and that the colour blends or contrasts well with the flowers you are using. Also consider the texture: delicate china or glass is lovely for light spring flowers, and wicker is perfect for an arrangement with grasses. I often arrange my flowers in a basket, as the texture and colour seem to blend better with dried flowers than does china.

You can often recycle broken, chipped, or otherwise damaged china. Some of my most successful containers are often the least expensive – little pots covered with moss, a glass jar covered in leaves tied with raffia.

Finishing touches
A few simple finishing touches can make all the difference between an attractive arrangement and a professional-looking one. Neatly tied bows can give a very professional finish to a project. There are many different types of ribbon available, and you can find shops that specialize in ribbons alone. One of my favourite forms is twisted paper ribbon, which unfolds from a long, snake-like string into a wonderfully textured wide ribbon in an attractive range of colours. It is firm enough to hold its shape well, but flexible enough to be tied easily.

In addition to ordinary silk ribbons, you can also use wired ribbon to make very effective, well-presented bows. I like to make four-looped bows (see page 124). Starched fabric bows can be made out of inexpensive cotton sheeting (see page 123), then sprayed in gold, silver or whatever colour you require.

The size of the bow is an important element in the overall design of the arrangement. If in doubt, err on the generous side, particularly if the arrangement is fairly simple – as in the Lavender Pots on page 69 or the Larkspur Bowl on page 51. Bows can also be used to hide any oasis that protrudes above the neck of the container; for this you will need a wide ribbon, such as twisted paper or wired silk. Whatever type you use, choose a colour that goes with the flowers in your arrangement.

In each of the arrangements in this book, I have specified the quantity and kind of flowers that I have used. If the same flowers are not available in your area, look for ones that have a similar colour, shape, and texture. It is these qualities that are important rather than the type of flower. In other words, if I have used pink roses and you can only get hold of red ones, do not change the overall colour scheme. Buy pink carnations or pink peonies instead, which will produce much the same effect.

Remember that the projects in this book are only my suggestions. The real pleasure of creating dried flower arrangements comes from experimenting with different colours and shapes and discovering what you like. So feel free to try out your own ideas. Above all, enjoy it!

Here is a selection of the many different shapes that dried flower arrangements can take, including some of the most popular, such as garlands, wreaths, and swags. Always try to use flowers that suit the overall form of the arrangement, and keep the colour and the form simple, not fussy. Clockwise from top left: Christmas Door Wreath (page 106); Christmas Garland (page 110); Harvest Swag (page 84); Shelf Arrangement (page 81); Wheatsheaf (page 78); Architectural Arrangement with Roses (page 88); Summer Hat (page 62); Topiary Rose Trees (page 48).

Drying Flowers

OF ALL THE METHODS for drying flowers, air drying is the most commonly used for almost all types of flowers, and the easiest. The secret to successful drying is to dry the flowers as quickly as possible after they have been picked, making sure that the air circulates around them, so that they don't become mouldy and rot before they dry. An airing rack fixed to the kitchen ceiling works well, but if you have a large airy cupboard, you will find that the darkness helps to preserve the colour of the flowers. The drier the place, the quicker and better the flowers will dry, and a little warmth also helps to speed up the process.

The weight and texture of the different types of flowers determine whether you dry them hanging upside down, flat on a drying rack made of chicken wire, or upright in a vase. Twisting climbers, like hops or clematis, can be dried by twining them around a bamboo pole. Cones can be dried in a bowl and make an attractive decoration in their own right while doing so. Flowers with heavy seed heads dry better if supported on an open-mesh rack made of chicken wire nailed to a wooden box.

Silica gel is the best way to preserve flowers with soft petals. They can then be used as decoration, glued into the arrangement, as the stems will probably be too delicate to be wired. Silica-gel-dried flowers are particularly fragile and lose their colour quickly if the atmosphere is even slightly damp. My own favourite use for them is on top of potpourri. An ideal way to use dessicant-dried flowers is as a flower picture, where they are protected by the glass. It is also possible to dry some flowers successfully in a microwave oven (see page 16).

It is important that all flowers to be dried are picked at the right time, when they are just coming into bloom. If they are faded or past their best, they will not look good when dried. (See the charts on page 17 for a guide as to what to pick when.)

Remember that flowers shrink as they dry because they lose the moisture that makes up a large part of their content. The drying process also makes the plants more inclined to be brittle, although much of the brittleness can be avoided if the plants are not over-dried. It is best to use the more delicate flowers as accents in your dried flower arrangements, and to use the stronger, more easily dried flowers to provide the bulk.

The length of time that each bunch takes to dry varies according to the type of flower, the heat of the room, and the density of the bunch, but normally allow 7 to 14 days. Test for dryness by touching the flowers: if they are dry and the stems are rigid, they are ready to use or can be stored away.

Natural drying

Plants with woody stems can be allowed to dry naturally and upright in a jug, as they are self-supporting and the stems will not bend or droop. A little water in the base of the jug helps them to dry out at the appropriate rate. Make sure the jug is kept in a room with an even, warm temperature, but do not stand it in bright sunlight as the colours of the flowers will fade.

Place the flowers upright in a jug with $\frac{1}{4}$ in (1.5 cm) of water. They will take roughly 10 days to dry. Among the flowers suitable for this method are hydrangeas and gypsophila.

Drying heavy-headed flowers

To dry heavy-headed flowers such as allium heads, artichokes, and thistles, make a simple rack out of chicken wire stapled to a cardboard box and insert the stalks of the flowers. They will normally dry in about one week.

Air drying

Use a laundry drying rack or hang up several bamboo poles some distance from the ceiling to allow room for the stems of the flowers. Wire the flowers into suitably sized bunches and hang them upside down from the poles about 10 in (25 cm) apart to allow the air to circulate. Hang away from steam or dampness.

The drying rack in my kitchen is always full of flowers in different stages of the drying process and makes a wonderful decorative feature. Once they have dried completely, I take them down and store them, leaving space for the next harvest of flowers.

Drying on a bamboo pole

1 Strip off any unwanted leaves and fasten the stems of the bunch of flowers to be dried with a strong elastic band – they shrink during drying and the band is needed to keep them in place (see inset picture). Using medium-gauge stub wire, thread the wire through the stems of the bunch of flowers, bind the stems a few times with the wire, and leave a long tail with which to hang the bunch.

2 Hang the bunches with enough space between them to allow the air to circulate. If the bunches are too close together, the flowers will disintegrate more easily.

Microwave drying

If you want to speed up the silica-gel technique, you can use a microwave oven. Make sure that the container is suitable for the microwave oven (i.e., non-metal and non-plastic). Cover the bottom of a suitable container with silica gel and arrange flowers as though for the normal silica-gel drying techniques (see opposite). Use a medium setting (about 300–350 watts). If available, also try the defrost setting (about 200 watts). Although you will have to experiment to determine exactly what temperatures and times to use, around 2 to $2\frac{1}{2}$ minutes for $\frac{1}{2}$ lb (250 g) is about normal. It is better to err on the side of caution and give the flowers less time. You can always repeat the procedure if they are not dry. Give the flowers you have dried some standing time – around 10 minutes for small delicate flowers to 30 minutes for flowers with large petals.

Glycerine drying

Many different kinds of leaves can be dried using glycerine, which also helps to keep glossy leaves shiny, although the deep green may gradually fade. If you wish, you can dye glycerine-dried plants by adding a few drops of food colouring to the solution, which will be soaked up by the stems and petals, changing their colour. Replenish the solution if it evaporates,

Make a few diagonal cuts in the stems and place them in a solution of equal amounts of boiling water and glycerine. Stand the jug in a dark place; absorption usually takes 2 to 3 weeks.

Silica-gel drying

Silica gel is a useful method for drying flowers with very delicate petals, such as pansies, zinnias, anemones, narcissi and other spring flowers. To keep re-using the crystals, heat them in a shallow dish in a warm oven, then store them in an airtight container.

1 Place the silica-gel crystals in an airtight plastic container, filling it to a depth of about $\frac{1}{2}$ in (1.5 cm). Then lay the flower heads, face up, on top.

2 Using a spoon, gently push more crystals under the flowers, between them, and over them until they are covered completely. Take care not to crush or distort the petals. Seal the container.

3 Check after 2 or 3 days to see if they are dry. If so, remove them by carefully pouring off the silica-gel crystals. Clean the flowers with a soft paintbrush.

Storing dried flowers

One of the greatest advantages of dried flowers is that, provided you store them carefully, you can keep them for some time before using them. If you store dried flowers away from the light, they will keep their colour better and longer.

First and foremost, the flowers must be absolutely bone-dry before they are stored, otherwise they will rot. The place in which they are stored must also be dry.

Take care that the flowers are not crushed in the storing process, otherwise the stems and flower heads will become distorted. I normally keep mine in cardboard boxes with lids to keep the light out. Bunches of flowers that have been air dried can be laid carefully on tissue paper, with a tissue paper collar to protect the heads. Label and date the boxes, and use first those that have been stored the longest. Silica-gel-dried flowers keep best in an airtight plastic container.

Certain flowers such as peonies, which are prone to harbouring bugs, are best stored with a few mothballs. Otherwise you may find the flower heads have been eaten while in storage.

1 Lay some tissue paper in a large box. Start placing the flowers on the tissue paper. Using a twist of tissue paper, make a collar on which to rest the heads of the flowers.

2 Pack the flowers loosely into the box, and add a few mothballs to keep the flower heads from being eaten by bugs while in storage.

Good garden flowers for drying

The following are the flowers that I grow most successfully. There are lots of others that you can use, so do as I have done and experiment. On the whole, plants with fairly small flower heads and reasonably firm stems air dry very well. Plants with large waxy flowers or large soft petals often require silica-gel preservation. If you want to keep the shine on glossy leaves, try glycerine preservation methods.

Always make sure that you pick the flowers just before their peak of perfection. If they are going over, they will not dry well, whatever method you use.

If you develop a preference for certain kinds of flowers and they grow well in the climate in which you live, it is worthwhile setting aside a small area of the garden to growing them specifically for drying. Lavender, larkspur, achillea, and cornflowers are all easy to grow, and you will save yourself a great deal of money if you grow these from seed yourself.

WINTER

Box (*Buxus sempervirens*)
　leaves
Hebe sp.
Ivy (*Hedera* sp.) leaves **
Pine (*Pinus* sp.)

SPRING

Anemone sp. *
Beech (*Fagus sylvatica*)
　leaves **
Bluebell (*Endymion*
　non-scriptus)
Buttercup (*Ranunculus acris*)
Camellia sp. *
Clematis sp. *
Daffodil (*Narcissi* sp.) *
Eucalyptus sp. leaves **
Gentian (*Gentiana* sp.) *
Hellebore (*Helleborus* sp.) *
Hyacinth (*Hyacinthus* sp.)
　florets *
Iris sp. *
Mimosa (*Acacia longifolia*)
Oak (*Quercus* sp.) leaves **
Pansy (*Viola tricolor*) *
Primrose (*Primula* sp.) *
Rhododendron sp. *
Violet (*Viola* sp.) *

SUMMER

Achillea sp.
Alchemilla mollis

Allium sp., flowers
Anthemis sp.
Artemisia sp.
Safflower (*Carthamus* sp.)
Carnation (*Dianthus* sp.)
Cornflower (*Centaurea cyanus*)
Delphinium sp.
Golden rod (*Solidago*
　canadensis)
Gypsophila sp.
Helichrysum sp.
Larkspur (*Consolida ambigua*)
Lavender (*Lavandula* sp.)
Lily (*Lilium* sp.) *
Nigella sp.
Passion flower
　(*Passiflora* sp.) *
Peony (*Paeonia* sp.)
Roses (*Rosa* sp.)

FALL

Allium sp., seed heads
Chrysanthemum sp.
Cyclamen sp. *
Dahlia sp.
Grasses
Marigold (*Tagetes* sp.)
Poppy seed heads
　(*Papaver* sp.)

* Suitable for silica-gel
preservation
** Suitable for glycerine
preservation

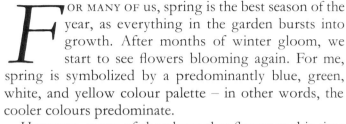

SPRING

*Arrangements for spring need to be light, delicate, and airy, in keeping with
the types of plants available at this time of year.*

OR MANY OF US, spring is the best season of the
year, as everything in the garden bursts into
growth. After months of winter gloom, we
start to see flowers blooming again. For me,
spring is symbolized by a predominantly blue, green,
white, and yellow colour palette – in other words, the
cooler colours predominate.

However, many of the plants that flower at this time
are not suitable for air drying, the easiest and most commonly used method of preserving flowers. Most spring
flowers, with their soft stems and waxy petals – in particular, bulbs like narcissi or hyacinths – are better suited
to preserving in silica gel (see page 16).

Other suitable flowers include winter-flowering pansies, camellia flowers, and different coloured hellebores.
You will see, on the following pages, that I have included
several different types of hellebore. Although I have not
used them in any of the projects in the book, they make
excellent individual place setting decorations, used with
some dried box, arranged in a small napkin ring filled
with oasis. The delicate little heads of the miniature
narcissus, 'Tête-à-Tête,' look much more effective
in small-scale arrangements than the bigger trumpet
daffodils.

To create a spring effect in flower arrangements, use
yellow, white, and green summer-dried flowers, adding
spring-flowering plants like narcissi, bluebells, or buttercups to bring an authentic seasonal touch. Use fresh-
looking greenery and light-coloured or see-through jars.

The different kinds of mosses available make a perfect
foil for the delicate flowers of the spring bulbs. If you
have a garden, you can often find flat moss growing on
stones or tiles, which you can peel off carefully and
preserve for your arrangements.

Most of my spring arrangements are fairly small-scale
because spring flowers do not come in such great quantities as summer- and autumn-flowering plants. The
garden in spring has a jewel-like quality about it with dots
of brilliant colour here and there. I try to echo this feeling
in my arrangements. The Spring Basket on page 24 has
small narcissi scattered over it, and the Spring Garden on
page 36 has little flowers sprinkled in the grass.

When creating arrangements, I take the flowers that I
would like to use as the starting point. I can achieve a far
more satisfactory result that way than by thinking of a
shape first, and then trying to find the flowers to fit it.

Spring Flowers

Although they are quite fragile, the delicate, waxy blooms of most spring bulbs, and in particular of hellebores, dry well in silica gel.

Narcissi 'Solidor'

Bluebells
(*Endymion non-scriptus*)

Hellebores (*Helleborus* sp.)

Pansies
(*Viola tricolor*)

Narcissi 'Tête-à-Tête'

Anemone sp.

Anemone sp.

Mimosa
(*Acacia longifolia*)

Buttercups
(*Ranunculus acris*)

Pansies
(*Viola tricolor*)

Hellebores
(*Helleborus* sp.)

Pansies
(*Viola tricolor*)

Hellebores
(*Helleborus* sp.)

Camellia sp.

Spring Basket

Spring is associated with the bright yellows and blues of flowers like daffodils,
tulips, and scillas. Although these spring flowers cannot be air dried,
they can be preserved in silica gel and glued to the finished arrangement.

FLOWERS

½ bunch golden rod (*Solidago canadensis*)
½ bunch *Ammobium alatum grandiflorum* (dyed)
10 daffodils (small-flowered *Narcissus* sp., previously dried in silica gel – see page 16)
Quail's eggs (or others)

A BASKET MAKES AN IDEAL GIFT if you fill it with eggs of one kind or another. I filled mine with quail's eggs, simply because they are so attractive, but foil-covered chocolate eggs would look equally pretty. As a present for children, replace the oasis with a large chocolate egg partially hidden in the moss and add tiny foil-covered ones for decoration.

The basket is relatively easy to decorate. Make up the little bunches of golden rod first and then attach all the bunches to the basket. The secret is to make up the bunches in the same way that a florist creates a bouquet – put the longest stems underneath and graduate the flower heads downwards. Handle the daffodils with great care – flowers dried in silica gel are very fragile.

I bought a small wicker basket with a handle, but if yours does not have one, you can make it out of twigs.

MATERIALS

Basket about 6 in (15 cm) in diameter
Flat moss
Oasis
Fine-gauge stub wire
Reel wire
Silver birch twigs (for handle, if required)

When creating a pretty design like this basket, keep the colour palette simple or it will be too busy. I limited the colours here to yellow and green to give it unity.

Making a twig handle

Birch twigs are a good choice for a handle as they are very flexible. Select 12 twigs of roughly the same length – about 12 in (30 cm) – or trim them accordingly.

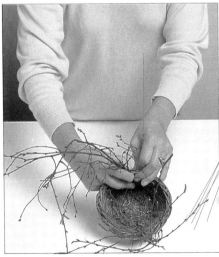

1 Make 2 bunches of 6 or so twigs, and wire to opposite sides of the basket edge. Thread stub wire through the basket from the front and twist tightly around each bunch.

2 Join the bunches together to form a handle, twisting them together and then binding them with reel wire.

3 Twist any straggling pieces of twig into the handle. Cover the wire with raffia if you wish.

Small-flowered daffodils
(*Narcissus* sp.)

Golden rod
(*Solidago
canadensis*)

Quail's eggs

*Ammobium
alatum
grandiflorum* (dyed)

Flat moss

Creating the arrangement

1 Make small bunches of golden rod from the florets, positioning them to make a slightly elongated bunch, and wire with reel wire, leaving a 4 in (10 cm) tail of wire.

2 Attach the bunches of golden rod to the rim of the basket with the wire, laying the head of each new bunch over the stems of the previous one.

3 Attach the bunches to the handle as well. Then, using a long reel of wire, bind lightly over the bunches through the basket all around the rim to neaten the effect. Do not pull the wire too tightly.

4 Using a glue gun (see page 120), glue the ammobium heads to the rim of the basket and around the handle in small groups of 4 to 5 at evenly spaced intervals.

5 Handling them with care as they are very delicate, glue the daffodils to the arrangement wherever there is a suitable space on the handle and the rim.

6 Fill the basket with oasis (you can use up odd pieces left over from other arrangements) or crumpled paper, cover with flat moss, and add the eggs as the final decoration.

Fireplace Arrangement

A light and sunny arrangement helps to create a splash of colour in an empty hearth.
This arrangement relies on yellows, blue, and gold for a spring look.

FLOWERS

½ bunch sea lavender
(*Goniolimon tartaricum*)

4 heads *Hydrangea arborescens*
'Annabelle'

2 bunches golden rod
(*Solidago canadensis*)

1 bunch *Achillea ptarmica*
'The Pearl'

2 bunches larkspur
(*Consolida ambigua*)

2 bunches red mini spray roses

1 bunch *Achillea filipendulina*
'Coronation Gold'

2 bunches globe thistle
(*Echinops ritro*)

2 bunches *Centaurea macrocephala*

A FIREPLACE WITHOUT A FIRE burning in the grate can look very bleak. Late spring is the ideal time to create an arrangement that fills the hearth with colour. Although many spring flowers are not really sufficiently bulky to make an arrangement large and tall enough for this purpose, by using summer flowers in yellows, blues, and greens you can create a very spring-like look.

Fireplaces vary in size, and you will have to work out what shape you need for the space you are trying to fill. You will almost certainly have to adjust the arrangement once it is in position, but try not to spoil the basic shape. The sides of the arrangement should overlap the edges of the fireplace a little, so avoid making the arrangement too tall and thin. Aim for balance in the width and the height; it will look far more generous. Remember that the arrangement will also be seen from the sides, so make sure that these are well filled.

MATERIALS

Basket (roughly
12 × 6 in/30 × 15 cm)

Oasis (size of basket plus
1 in/3 cm additional depth)

The arrangement for the fireplace has to be finished off in situ, so that you can fill any holes and adjust the overall shape to fit the space available. You can use any faded flowers for bulking up the arrangement at the back. They will not be seen, but will prevent the arrangement from looking too airy.

Gauging stem length

Experienced arrangers can snip off the flower stems to the correct length by
eye. Novices will probably need to check the length first.

1 Hold the stem head down against the part of the arrangement where it is to be placed and add an extra 1 in (2.5 cm) to the length for insertion into the oasis. Snip the stem at that point.

2 If you cut a stem too short by mistake, you can lengthen it by twisting medium-gauge stub wire two or three times around the base, leaving a tail of wire to provide a stem.

Creating the arrangement

1 Wedge large pieces of oasis firmly into the basket, leaving 1 in (2.5 cm) above the rim. Insert the sea lavender to form the basic skeleton. Try it in the fireplace to check that it fits the shape.

2 Add the 4 hydrangea heads to the front and sides of the arrangement, with about 4–5 in (10–12 cm) of stem above the oasis.

3 The golden rod goes in next. Open out the bunches and fluff up the flower heads to help give them bulk. Golden rod is a very good filler, but the florist's bunches are usually packed too tightly.

4 Finish positioning the golden rod, inserting it between the hydrangea and sea lavender, making an even spread.

Hydrangea arborescens
'Annabelle'

Sea lavender
Goniolimon tartaricum

Globe thistle
(*Echinops ritro*)

Golden rod
(*Solidago canadensis*)

Mini spray roses

5 Insert the white achillea in small unwired bunches – 3 stems to a bunch. Position the flower heads so that they are level; snip the base of the stems. Spread the achillea evenly around the arrangement.

6 Add the larkspur. Strip off any crooked shoots, and make small bunches of 2 to 3 heads, trimmed level, as in step 5. There is no need to wire them; the larkspur stems are firm enough.

7 Add mini spray roses and yellow achillea for additional colour. Distribute them evenly around the arrangement.

8 Next insert the echinops. This adds shape and texture to the arrangement. The yellow centaurea goes in last, using 4 to 5 stems in a block.

Achillea filipendulina
'Coronation Gold'

Centaurea macrocephala

Achillea ptarmica
'The Pearl'

Larkspur
(*Consolida ambigua*)

9 Finally, check the arrangement in situ, adding colour where needed and ensuring that there are no holes.

Arrangement in a Glass Bowl

Fresh light colours combine well with glass containers for attractive spring arrangements. These buttercups and bluebells, combined with yellow roses, are set off against a background of feathery lunaria.

MATERIALS

Glass bowl (with neck)
Glazed chintz – about $\frac{1}{2}$ yd (50 cm) square
Oasis
Satin ribbon
Reel wire

FLOWERS

1 bunch *Lunaria minima*
5 bunches bluebells (*Endymion non-scriptus*)
5 bunches buttercups (*Ranunculus acris*)
2 bunches *Chrysanthemum* sp.
10 yellow roses

SPRING IS USUALLY associated with the yellows, whites, and blues of many of the flowers, and the fresh green of young foliage. This arrangement would make a good table centre decoration and should look good from all sides. Turn the arrangement frequently as you insert the flowers to make sure that it is well balanced. To make it easier, you can use a turn-table or a revolving cheese board.

One of the principles I adhere to in making dried flower arrangements is to avoid holes – in other words, I try to ensure that no daylight is visible through the arrangement. The effect of this is to strengthen the colours. It also pays to keep the colour and flower combinations relatively simple, as this makes them appear stronger.

I have used plain green glazed chintz to fill a clear glass bowl because I like the light, spring-like effect. You could, of course, use a different coloured fabric in the bowl and vary the colours of the arrangement, but it helps to create a feeling of uniformity if the ribbon and the chintz pick up the colours of the dried flowers.

The lunaria, chrysanthemums, and roses can all be bought in florists' shops. I picked the bluebells and buttercups at a friend's farm and dried them myself.

As in all dried flower arrangements, the proportions are an important element of the design. In this case, the tallest flowers are about one and a half times the depth of the bowl.

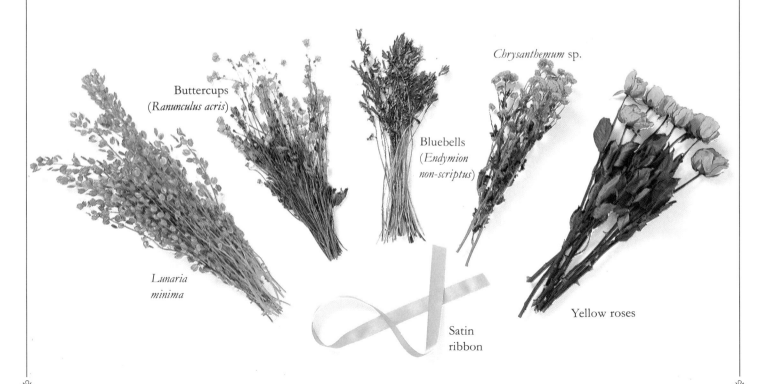

Buttercups
(*Ranunculus acris*)

Chrysanthemum sp.

Bluebells
(*Endymion non-scriptus*)

Lunaria
minima

Satin
ribbon

Yellow roses

Creating the arrangement

1 Take the four corners of the fabric and scrunch it into a rough ball shape. Press it into the neck of the bowl and smooth out.

2 Leave ¾ in (20 mm) of fabric above the neck of the bowl. Insert the oasis, leaving about 1 in (25 mm) above the neck.

3 Insert the lunaria stems into the oasis as shown, starting with the tallest. Trim the others to make a semicircular arc.

4 Fill in with bunches of bluebells and buttercups, aiming to get an even spread of blue and yellow throughout the arrangement. If the stalks are weak, wire 5 or 6 stems together.

5 Wrap the wire around the stem and insert the bunches into the oasis. Add the chrysanthemums to give bulk to the arrangement, stripping any surplus leaves off the stems.

6 Add the yellow roses, steamed open (see page 58), distributing them evenly around the arrangement. Fill in any holes by "floating" more flowers – in other words, allow them to be supported by the rest of the arrangement.

7 Check the base for any holes and fill in. Tie a satin ribbon with the same texture on both sides, or a cord, in a bow around the neck of the jar, and trim the ends of the ribbon or cord neatly.

Top-of-cupboard Arrangement

The top of a cupboard or wardrobe is an ideal place for this type of arrangement. If your cupboard has a lip at the top, as this one does, use a fairly deep container or stand the container on something to raise it up so that all of the arrangement will be in view.

MATERIALS

Oasis (9 in/23 cm long ×
4½ in/11 cm wide × 3 in/
8 cm deep)

Oasis tray

Florist's oasis tape or
rubber band

FLOWERS

5 heads *Hydrangea macrophylla*

2 bunches golden rod
(*Solidago canadensis*)

1 bunch safflower
(*Carthamus tinctorius*)

½ bunch dudinea
(*Dodonaea viscosa*)

2 bunches *Chrysanthemum* sp.

½ bunch *Achillea filipendulina*
'Coronation Gold'

THE ADVENT OF SPRING encourages even the most haphazard housekeeper to clean the house. What better time to make an attractive arrangement for any relatively high, broad surface, such as a wardrobe or the top of a tall cupboard?

If you are making an arrangement for a position higher than eye level, you will need to consider the angle from which it is viewed. Since the base of the arrangement will be the most visible part, it has to be really well filled. To achieve this, it helps if the arrangement is placed on the table and you sit on the floor, so that you view it from below as you work on it.

Because the arrangement is high up, it needs to be fairly bright in colour; otherwise it will fail to make any impact. For most situations, it is also better if the arrangement is wider than it is tall. If you have several cupboards, a matching pair would look attractive.

Overleaf: Vibrant, contrasting colours work well here, because the décor is fairly plain and provides a good foil for a brightly coloured arrangement. Add more flowers if needed once the arrangement is in position.

Safflower
(*Carthamus tinctorius*)

Hydrangea macrophylla

Chrysanthemum sp.

Achillea filipendulina
'Coronation Gold'

Dudinea
(*Dodonaea viscosa*)

Golden rod
(*Solidago canadensis*)

Creating the arrangement

1 Put the oasis on a tray and secure it with tape or a rubber band. Insert the hydrangea heads to create a fan shape, 1 head on top of the oasis, 1 at either end, and 2 in front.

2 Bulk up the arrangement with golden rod, making sure that the majority of the flower heads are facing forwards and pointing down to help fill the lower part of the arrangement.

3 Use the carthamus in bunches of 3 heads to fill in between the hydrangea and golden rod. Make sure they also point down, and check that they are no higher than the tallest hydrangea head.

4 Insert the dudinea, again concentrating on the lower half of the arrangement and ensuring that you achieve an even spread of colour throughout the arrangement.

5 Insert the button chrysanthemums in small bunches. Make sure the colour of these, too, is distributed evenly so that the arrangement looks good from any angle.

6 Insert the achillea to create splashes of bright colour where needed to brighten up the arrangement and to help fill any holes. The aim is to achieve a solid mass of colour.

Spring Garden

Inspired by Japanese bonsai trees, this miniature spring garden is created from mimosa and golden rod.

MATERIALS

Container roughly 6 in (15 cm) long × 4 in (10 cm) wide
Block of oasis
3 apple twigs for "tree"
Rose wire
Flat moss
Large and small pebbles

FLOWERS

1 bunch golden rod (*Solidago canadensis*)
1 bunch mimosa (*Acacia longifolia*)
A few yellow button chrysanthemum heads

SOMETIMES VERY SIMPLE ARRANGEMENTS are the most effective. Although they require very little in the way of materials, they are often quite difficult to make well because they rely on having an excellent eye for proportion. With this particular arrangement, it is very important to make sure that the "branches" of the tree are not so large that they make the arrangement top-heavy.

Choose your container first, and then make sure that the "tree" part of the arrangement is not much taller than the length of the dish. The mimosa used for the branches is normally easy to find in florist's shops in spring. It is not cheap, but you do not need very much of it. You can dry it yourself quite easily, provided you dry it as quickly as possible.

The trunk of the tree was created from apple twigs, which are ideal because they are quite thick and have unusual gnarled shapes. I also collected a few pebbles from the beach to give a Japanese look to the garden part.

Japanese-looking in its simplicity, this spring garden with its mimosa and golden rod "tree" looks best in a very plain, spare setting, echoing its oriental inspiration.

Shaping the oasis

The flowers that form the branches of the "tree" are inserted into an oval of oasis. To make the oval you will need to cut it out from a block of oasis cut in half lengthwise.

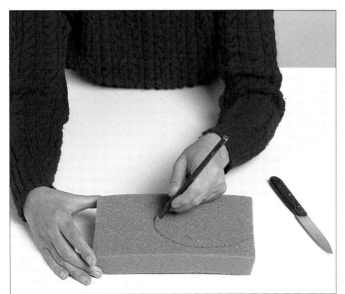

1 *With a pointed implement (a pencil will do), draw a neat oval shape on the oasis block. The indentation in the oasis will serve as a cutting guide.*

2 *Cut carefully around the drawn oval. It is easiest if you cut the oasis away in sections, slicing through it with a sharp kitchen knife.*

Creating the arrangement

1 Pack the container tightly with oasis. Sharpen each end of the apple twigs to a point using a sharp knife, and insert them into the oasis at one end of the container.

2 Wire small bunches of golden rod heads and insert them into the sides and top of the oasis oval. Try to keep the shape elongated and rather flat on top.

3 Fill the top and sides of the oval with golden rod, so that it resembles the branches of a tree in flower. You do not need to wire the golden rod used to fill the arrangement – simply push the stems into the oasis.

Mimosa (*Acacia longifolia*)

Apple twigs

4 *Impale the decorated oasis on the twigs, gluing it firmly in place if necessary. Snip off small sprigs of mimosa and insert them into the oasis oval.*

5 *Cut the moss to cover the top of the container, and press it down firmly into the oasis. Secure with "hairpins" of wire at intervals along the oasis.*

Golden rod
(*Solidago canadensis*)

Chrysanthemum sp.

Flat moss

Pebbles

6 *Around the base of the tree add a few pebbles and several heads of yellow chrysanthemums, the stems of which can be pushed straight into the oasis.*

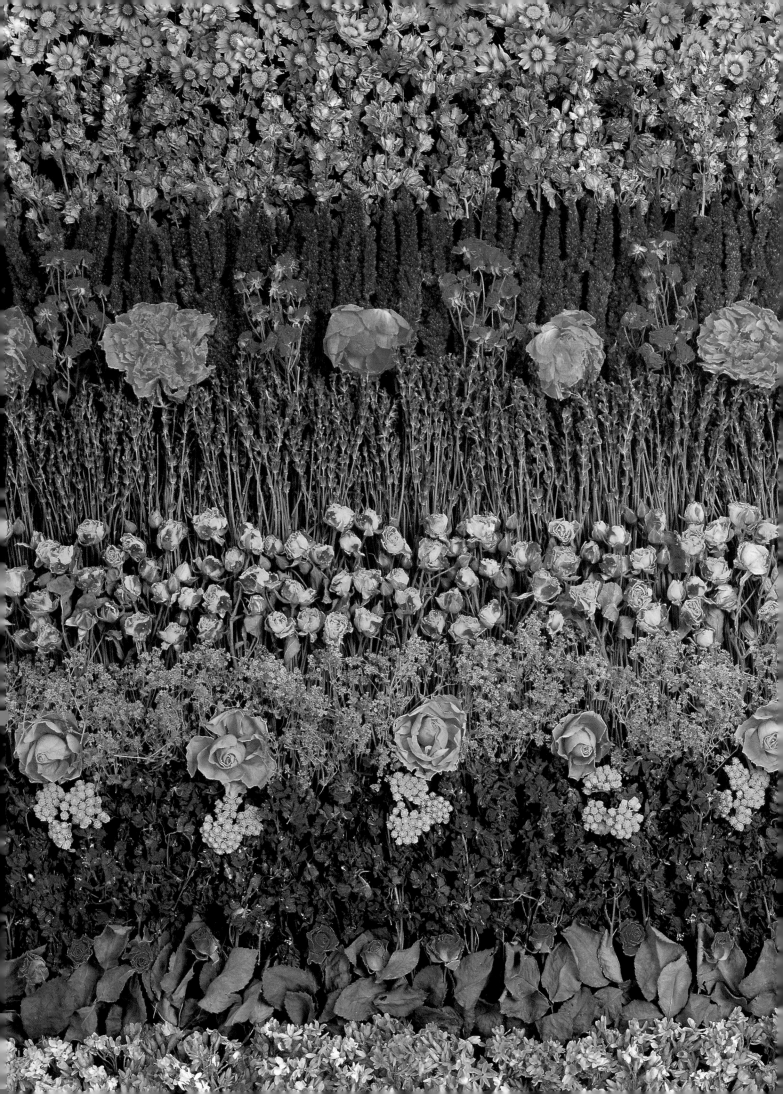

SUMMER

This is the most prolific season for flowers suitable for drying, with a great selection to choose from. In fact, you will find it difficult to keep up with what comes into bloom!

IF YOU WANT TO GROW FLOWERS in your own garden for dried flower arrangements, then it is best to opt for the ones that dry well and easily. Yarrow (*Achillea* sp.) is easy to grow and dries very well, as do larkspur (*Consolida ambigua*) and cornflowers (*Centaurea cyanus*). Gypsophila, helichrysum, and limonium are other good subjects for the border and for drying, as are love-in-a-mist and lavender, stachys and alchemilla. Peonies can be air dried with great success, and the flowers of old-fashioned roses dry wonderfully well in silica gel.

The trouble with growing flowers specifically for drying is that you really need to set aside an area of the garden, rather like the vegetable garden, for this purpose – otherwise your borders will suffer from being stripped of their flowers at the best time of year. Professional growers raise them in long strips like vegetables, and there is nothing to prevent you from doing the same. In fact, a friend of mine grows larkspur and cornflowers in rows or blocks among the vegetables. It cheers up the vegetable garden no end.

If you are growing flowers for drying, then do be sure to stake the taller, more delicate ones, such as delphiniums. In dried flower arranging, it is vital to have the straightest stems possible, and an efficient staking system will ensure that the flowers are in peak condition when you come to pick them.

The hot weather in summer causes the flowers to go past their best quickly. Try to pick them in the early morning before the flower buds have fully opened and before the sun has done its work. To prevent mould and rot, make sure that any drops of water are shaken off before you bunch them up.

I associate the hot colours – oranges, pinks, reds, and mauves – with summer and certain flowers seem to me to be essential for summer arrangements. Roses, peonies, larkspur, marjoram, and lavender are all among my favourites. Dominant colours need to be contrasted with equally strong colours, and I tend to put reds with deep blues and mauves or rich yellows. Another option is to use several shades of similar colours for a striking effect, with reds, pinks, and mauves used together.

Summer Flowers

High summer offers a wealth of flowers. Here are some of the best, ranging from the deep blues and dark reds to the warm pinks and golds to the whites, silvers, and greens.

Larkspur
(*Consolida ambigua*)

Thyme
(*Thymus* sp.)

Cornflower
(*Centaurea cyanus*)

Peony
(*Paeonia lactiflora*)

Statice
(*Limonium sinuatum*)

Mint flower
(*Monarda didyma*)

Monkshood
(*Aconitum paniculatum*)

Lavender
(*Lavandula angustifolia* 'Hidcote')

Ageratum sp.

Delphinium
(*Delphinium elatum*)

Clary sage
(*Salvia horminum*)

Marjoram
(*Origanum vulgare*)

Carnation
(*Dianthus caryophyllus*)

Hybrid tea rose
(*Rosa* 'Mercedes')

Gayfeather
(*Liatris spicata*)

Rat's tail statice
(*Psylliostachys soworowii*)

Yarrow
(*Achillea millefolium*)
cultivars

Love-lies-bleeding
(*Amaranthus* sp.)

Astilbe sp.

Polygonum sp.

Clary sage
(*Salvia horminum*)

Polyanthus rosa
(*Rosa paleander* 'Joy')

Cornflower
(*Centaurea cyanus*)

Rhodanthe
(*Heipterum manglesii*)

Celosia cockscomb
(*Celosia argentea cristata*)

Silene sp.

The warmer colours of the spectrum — pinks, reds, oranges, golds, and yellows — have a distinctly summery feel. Of all the summer flowers, roses are probably the most evocative of this time of year; those shown here are just a small selection of the many kinds available.

Hybrid tea rose
(*Rosa* 'Tennessee')

Hybrid tea rose
(*Rosa* 'Rosario')

Hybrid tea rose
(*Rosa* 'Sonia')

Peony
(*Paeonia lactiflora*)

Larkspur
(*Consolida ambigua*)

Dudinea
(*Dodonaea viscosa*),
dyed

Polyanthus rose
(*Rose paleander*
'Dorius Rijkers')

Hybrid tea rose
(*Rosa* 'Kiss')

Hybrid tea rose
(*Rosa*
'La Minuette')

Globe amaranth
(*Gomphrena globosa*)

Polyanthus rose
(*Rosa paleander*
'Gloria Mundi')

Hybrid tea rose
(*Rosa* 'Golden Times')

Statice
(*Limonium sinuatum*)

Craspedia globosa

Jerusalem sage
(*Phlomis fruticosa*)

Polyanthus rose
(*Rosa paleander*
'La Rumba')

Giant scabious
(*Cephalaria gigantica*)

Yarrow
(*Achillea*
'Moonshine')

Chrysanthemum
(*Dendranthema × grandiflorum*)

Feverfew
(*Tanacetum parthenium*)

Curry plant
(*Helichrysum italicum*)

*Ammobium
alatum*, dyed

Hybrid tea rose
(*Rosa* 'Gerdo')

Lady's mantle
(*Alchemilla mollis*)

Yarrow
(*Achillea filipendulina*
'Coronation Gold')

Everlasting
(*Helichrysum* sp.)

Chamomile
(*Chamaemelum
nobile*), dyed

Lonas inodora

The silver, white, cream, and green flowers that you harvest in summer are particularly useful for filling arrangements and for giving an instant lift to an arrangement that has started to fade a little.

Lady's mantle
(*Alchemilla mollis*)

Love-lies-bleeding
(*Amaranthus* sp.)

Carthamus tinctorius

Lunaria thlaspe arvensis

Artemisia 'Powis Castle'

Knotted majoram
(*Origanum marjorana*)

Silver cypress

Meadow rue
(*Thalictrum* sp.)

'Ambrosiaia'
(*Chenopodium botrys*)

Bupleurum sp.

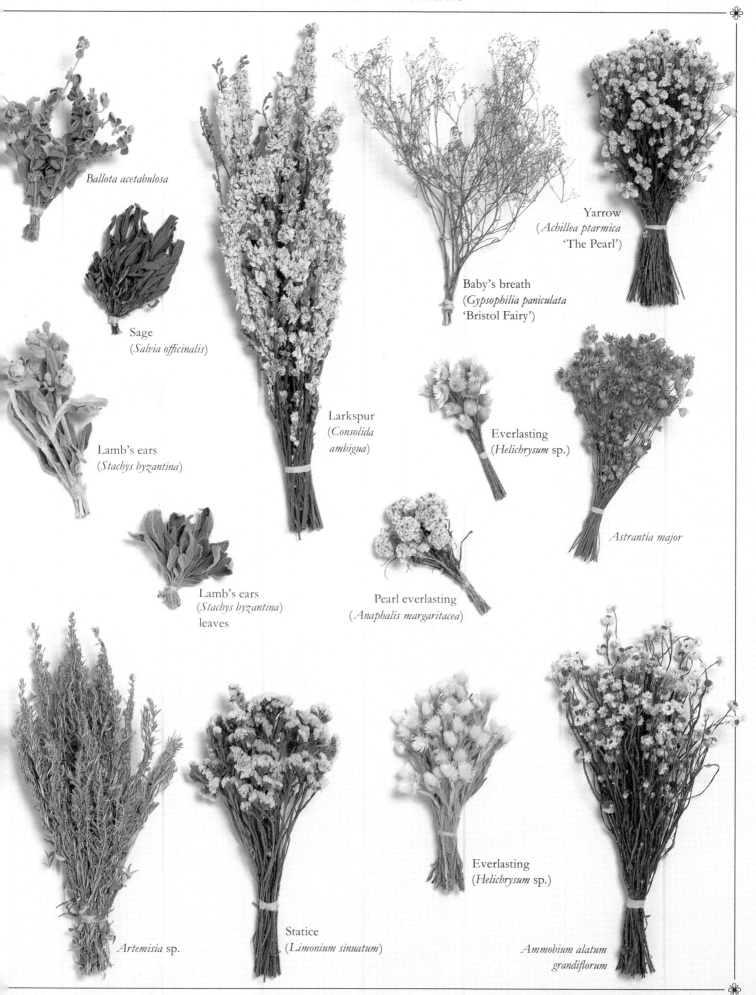

Ballota acetabulosa

Sage
(*Salvia officinalis*)

Lamb's ears
(*Stachys byzantina*)

Lamb's ears
(*Stachys byzantina*)
leaves

Larkspur
(*Consolida
ambigua*)

Baby's breath
(*Gypsophilia paniculata*
'Bristol Fairy')

Yarrow
(*Achillea ptarmica*
'The Pearl')

Everlasting
(*Helichrysum* sp.)

Astrantia major

Pearl everlasting
(*Anaphalis margaritacea*)

Artemisia sp.

Statice
(*Limonium sinuatum*)

Everlasting
(*Helichrysum* sp.)

Ammobium alatum
grandiflorum

Topiary Rose Trees

Elegant and simple, these rose trees are easy to make. Mine are about 9 in (23 cm) tall, but you can make smaller or bigger versions if you prefer.

MATERIALS

Oasis (including a ready-made ball, cut in half)
Medium-gauge stub wire
Plaster of Paris
Flat moss
3 in (7.5 cm) terracotta pot

FLOWERS

40 dark red roses

ROSES ARE among the most satisfying dried flowers to work with as they have deep rich colours and wonderful form. Use them to create jewel-like splashes of colour in a mixed flower arrangement or on their own, as I have here, to create these elegant little trees. I have used dark red roses because I think that the arrangement gains from using a deep colour.

The inspiration for this pair of rose trees came from my own garden, where I have a clipped holly tree that has a similar outline – a definite mushroom shape rather than the more usual round ball.

To anchor the stems in the pot, I used plaster of Paris rather than oasis. Because this is a fairly top-heavy structure, the base must be solid. However, plaster of Paris dries very fast, so you must work quickly. Insert slivers of oasis into the pot first to prevent the pot from cracking, as the plaster expands when it sets. Since the rose heads need to be reasonably full, you may need to steam them open before you start (see page 58).

If you wish to make a pair of these rose trees, as I have, then double the quantities of materials listed left.

These little rose trees make ideal end-pieces for a shelf or mantelpiece. I often put mine on a dresser, where they echo the colours in the china.

Dark red roses

Rose leaves

Flat moss

Creating the arrangement

1 Strip the leaves and thorns off the rose stems and set a few leaves aside. Remove the heads from 12 roses, leaving a $\frac{3}{4}$ in (2 cm) stalk. Wire the stems together to make a "trunk".

2 Prepare the base by inserting slivers of oasis around the inner edge of the pot. Cover the hole in the base of the pot with another small piece of oasis.

3 Mix the plaster of Paris and fill the pot to within 1 in (2.5 cm) of the rim. Set the trunk in the centre of the pot immediately, and hold it until the plaster is firm (about 5 minutes).

4 Wedge the base of the half-circle of oasis securely onto the top of the trunk. Start adding the rose heads to the half-circle of oasis, starting at the crown and working down.

5 Finish adding the roses to the oasis, making sure that they are close together with each stem pushed in firmly.

6 Steam the reserved rose leaves flat (see page 62). Lift off the oasis and glue the leaves to the base with the tips protruding.

7 Put a dab of glue on the top of the trunk and replace the oasis. Cover the base with moss and glue it in place.

Larkspur Bowl

This is one of my favourite arrangements. The colour is vibrant and intense, and it looks particularly good in a blue and white china jar.

MATERIALS
Large tobacco jar

Oasis

Wired silk ribbon

FLOWERS
15 bunches dark blue larkspur
(*Consolida ambigua*)

THIS IS AN EXTREMELY SIMPLE arrangement with just one principal ingredient. I think it looks most effective in a blue and white china tobacco jar. (I have often been able to buy ones with a chipped rim or a crack very cheaply in second-hand shops and markets.) The larkspur itself is quite tall, so the jar needs to be fairly large to prevent the arrangement from looking top-heavy.

In order to be sure that the larkspur is distributed evenly around the arrangement, you may find it helpful to use a turntable or a revolving cheeseboard.

If you wish, you could make a similar arrangement with a different single flower. However, you'll need a plant that has spires of flowers, such as lavender, rather than flowers at the end of the stem, in order to create the fullness and density of colour that are the chief attraction of the arrangement.

It is very important to insert the lowest stems at right angles to the pot, so make sure a narrow collar of oasis protrudes about 4½ in (11 cm) above the rim of the jar. A wired silk ribbon, tied in a bow, conceals the oasis.

Overleaf: The larkspur looks very effective on a side table – perhaps in a foyer or hall. Because it is fairly imposing – about 36 in (90 cm) high and 24 in (60 cm) wide – it needs to stand alone.

Larkspur (*Consolida ambigua*)   Wired silk ribbon

Creating the arrangement

1 Fill the bottom of the jar with crumpled newspaper and bits of broken oasis, then wedge a block of oasis into the neck of the jar. Insert the larkspur in small bunches of 3 to 4 stems into the top and sides of the oasis to create the framework for the width.

2 Start to build up the skeleton, inserting the larkspur fairly evenly on both the top and sides of the arrangement. The top and side pieces should be about the same length. Trim off any uneven parts of the flower heads.

3 Finish filling the oasis with larkspur; make sure there are no holes or gaps. Neaten it up, if necessary, by giving the arrangement a "hair cut" with a sharp pair of scissors.

4 Tie the wired silk ribbon in a neat four-looped bow (see page 124) around the neck of the tobacco jar to conceal the protruding oasis collar.

Welcome Wreath

Guests are often greeted with fresh flowers, but a welcome wreath on the door makes a pretty, and permanent, alternative. The rich deep reds and pinks look particularly warm and inviting.

FLOWERS

3 bunches lamb's ears (*Stachys byzantina*)
5 bunches marjoram (*Origanum vulgare*)
4 bunches sage (*Salvia officinalis*)
3 bunches clary sage (*Salvia horminum*)
3 heads *Hydrangea macrophylla*
4 bunches feverfew (*Tanacetum parthenium*)
6 bunches lavender (*Lavandula angustifolia* 'Hidcote')
2 bundles birch twigs, tied with raffia
5 red roses
18 bunches box (*Buxus sempervirens*)
9 bunches *Alchemilla mollis*
2 *Sterculia* pods
4 peonies (*Paeonia lactiflora*)
4 lotus seed heads (*Nelumbo lucifera*)

WREATHS CAN BE used for all kinds of situations. One of the nicest ideas is to make a welcome wreath for visitors, either fixed to the main entrance door or possibly to a guest-room door. In my own house, I hang wreaths on cupboard doors.

The colour combinations in this particular wreath appeal to me, and they are particularly suitable for a welcome wreath. Warm colours – reds, pinks, and mauves – are psychologically more welcoming than colder blues and greens. Texture is very important when making a wreath, and I like to include contrasts, such as the harder shapes of the bundles of birch twigs and the *Sterculia* pods with the more ethereal marjoram and hydrangea florets.

Herbs are particularly suitable for wreaths and offer the bonus of smelling nice. If you prefer, you can pick the herbs fresh from the garden and let them dry naturally in the wreath. The colours will fade eventually, but if kept out of direct sunlight the wreath should last for about two years, and some people find the softly faded colours more attractive than the new ones.

MATERIALS

Plastic-coated heavy-duty garden wire
Hay
Medium-gauge stub wire
Florists' mossing wire or green garden string
Rose wire

When making a wreath, you need a good solid base to work on. You can either use a ready-made wreath base or make your own. Cover it completely, ensuring that there are no holes or gaps, and no wires showing.

Making bunches of delicate flowers

Small bunches of more delicate flowers like alchemilla need to be wired as shown below with a tail-wire long enough to insert into the base of the arrangement.

1 *Lay four or five small branches with the heads together as shown. Bind the stems neatly with fine rose wire.*

2 *Using thicker stub wire, place one end across the bunch of stems. Wrap the free end around the stems three times.*

3 *Pull the free end down so that it forms a lengthened stem about 4 in (10 cm) long that can be inserted into the wreath.*

Creating the arrangement

Although the steps involved in constructing the wreath are photographed with the wreath laid flat, you may find it easier, once you have made the base, to work with the wreath hanging on a wall.

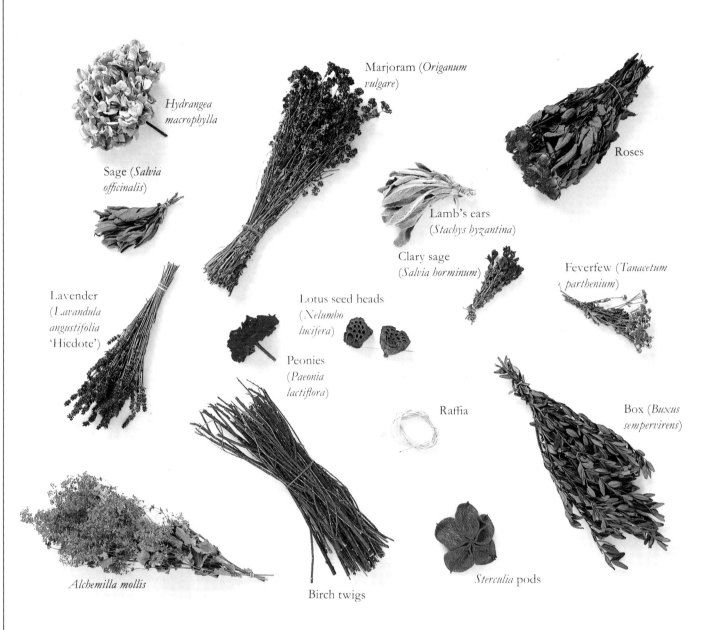

Hydrangea macrophylla

Marjoram (*Origanum vulgare*)

Roses

Sage (*Salvia officinalis*)

Lamb's ears (*Stachys byzantina*)

Clary sage (*Salvia horminum*)

Feverfew (*Tanacetum parthenium*)

Lavender (*Lavandula angustifolia* 'Hicdote')

Lotus seed heads (*Nelumbo lucifera*)

Peonies (*Paeonia lactiflora*)

Raffia

Box (*Buxus sempervirens*)

Alchemilla mollis

Birch twigs

Sterculia pods

1 Make a circle of heavy-duty wire about 12 in (30 cm) in diameter and fasten with stub wire. Make a long sausage shape of hay and place it on top of the wire circle. Bind the hay to the circle with mossing wire or green garden string.

2 Fold the hay over if necessary to create sufficient bulk. Fasten the ends of the wire and tuck them into the wreath base. Make a hook (see page 84).

3 Make up bunches of lamb's ears, marjoram, sage, clary sage, hydrangea, feverfew, lavender, birch twigs, and roses as shown on page 54.

4 Make up bunches of box with a wire stem, as shown on page 54. Attach the bunches in pairs at intervals around the wreath with the heads facing the same way.

5 Add the bunches of alchemilla in the same direction as the box. Then add the bunches of marjoram, covering the wire binding used for the bunches of box.

6 Add the bunches of sage to the sides of the wreath, again with the heads facing the same way as the bunches of box, alchemilla, and marjoram.

7 Add the florets of hydrangea, then the bunches of lamb's ears, and the bunches of lavender to complete the base decoration of the wreath. All should face in the same direction and cover the wires and stems of previous bunches.

8 Add the feverfew and clary sage. Place the birch twigs and sterculia pods on the wreath against the direction of the other plants. Glue on the roses, steamed-open peony flowers (see page 58), and lotus seed heads. Check for gaps, and fill accordingly.

A Pot of Roses

An ideal arrangement for a beginner, this little pot of dark red roses features a neat, geometric shape and the restricted use of colour.

MATERIALS

Small yoghurt pot
Plastic sheet with adhesive backing
Green raffia
Dry oasis
Florist's wire
Flat moss
Dyed green lichen moss

FLOWERS

20 heads *Nigella orientalis*
40 heads dark red roses

ONE OF THE most important rules for dried flower arrangements is to keep the colour palette limited and the form of the arrangement clearly defined. Watch the balance between the size of the arrangement and the pot. If you use too small a pot, the arrangement looks top-heavy and clumsy; if the pot is too large, the flowers look insignificant.

The use of only two kinds of flower – deep red roses and the starry heads of *Nigella orientalis* – makes an exciting use of form and texture, which contrasts well with the simple and inexpensive moss-covered pot. The softness of the pot also helps to offset the formality of the flower arrangement. This particular arrangement hangs on a useful trick – getting the tightly budded florist's roses to open out a little (see below).

A small formal arrangement like this elegant pot of roses can also be used as a table decoration for a buffet supper. Use a larger version for the main table and smaller ones for the individual tables.

Steaming flower buds open

Most flowers can be teased out from a tight bud into a looser shape. Carefully steam the heads, then gently press the outer petals open.

1 *Hold the flower head directly into the steam from the kettle, about 4 in (10 cm) from the spout, for a minute or so. Take care not to scald your hands.*

2 *Gently tease only the outer petals open using a piece of florist's wire. Take care not to touch the inner core of the flower, as it may disintegrate.*

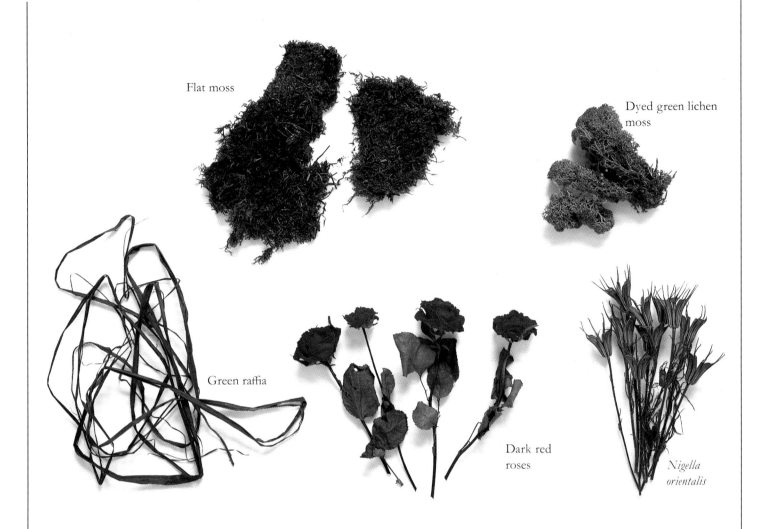

Flat moss

Dyed green lichen moss

Green raffia

Dark red roses

Nigella orientalis

Creating the arrangement

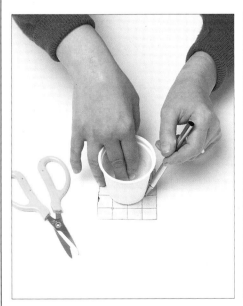

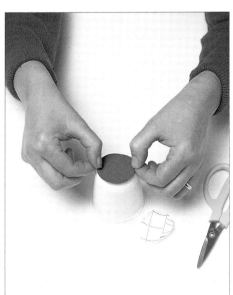

1 Put the plastic sheet face down on the table. Place the base of the pot in the centre and draw around it with a pencil.

2 Turn the pot upside down and put it to one side. Cut out the circle and peel off the backing layer.

3 Stick the circle of plastic to the base of the pot.

4 Take a block of oasis deep enough to fill the pot and to leave about $\frac{1}{2}$in (1.5 cm) above the rim. Press the pot on the oasis so that the rim leaves a visible mark.

5 With a sharp knife and using the impressed mark as a guide, slice the oasis until it fits the pot tightly.

6 Cut a piece of moss large enough to wrap around the sides of the pot. Use a glue gun to stick the moss to the sides of the pot.

7 Trim the surplus moss off each end of the pot until it covers the sides neatly. Pull the upper rim of moss out slightly at the upper sides of the pot to form a ridge.

8 Insert the first rose in the centre of the oasis to form the highest point of the domed arrangement.

9 Add the other roses, working from the centre out to the edges, trimming the stems as necessary. Add the nigella in random fashion, again working from the top of the dome downwards and outwards.

10 You will need to secure the moss around the base of the dome. Use short lengths of medium-gauge stub wire, and bend the wire in the centre.

11 Pin the pieces of moss under the dome of roses and nigella to create a neat edge between the moss pot and the flower arrangement.

12 Finally, tie a length of raffia or a ribbon around the centre of the moss pot, finishing with a neat bow.

Summer Hat

This is one of the easiest projects to make because you are working on a flat surface and can see exactly what you are doing at all times.

MATERIALS

Straw hat with wide brim
Reel wire

FLOWERS

Fern fronds (*Lupidium grosso* and *Adiantum* sp.)
20 stems pink larkspur (*Consolida ambigua*)
4 hydrangea florets (*Hydrangea macrophylla*)
4 peonies (*Paeonia lactiflora*)
11 roses with leaves (any small, dark red rose)

THIS PROJECT HAS TWO USES: you could wear it to a summer wedding or garden party, or simply hang it on the wall. It makes a particularly pretty decoration for a guest room or a girl's bedroom. Although I have chosen predominantly pink summer flowers, you could easily use a different colour scheme to suit your needs.

When planning the decoration for a hat, it is important to limit the number of colours and flowers. Too many different flowers and colours will look garish and overblown. Repeating the groups of colour and texture around the hat helps to unify it, which in turn makes it more elegant. To make sure that the decoration does not overwhelm the hat, keep it in scale with the size of the brim and crown.

The decoration is glued to the hat. I find a low-temperature glue gun is easiest to handle. Instructions for its use are given on page 120.

The finished hat, hanging on a door. I particularly like the combination of pinks, reds, and greens, but you can alter the colour scheme to suit the décor of the room or, if you are going to wear the hat, to match your outfit. Lavender, blue larkspur, peonies, and ferns would look pretty for a predominantly blue scheme.

Steaming leaves flat

The leaves of some dried flowers – roses, for example – are often very crinkled and curled. To decorate something flat, like a hat brim, it helps if they are first steamed fairly smooth.

1 Half-fill a kettle and bring it to boiling point. Hold the leaf stem in the steam for a few seconds, taking great care that your hands and arms are not scalded.

2 Put the still damp stem on a flat surface, and gently press each leaf flat with your fingers. Allow to dry for a few minutes before use.

Creating the arrangement

1 *Arrange the adiantum fern fronds around the hat, all facing in the same direction. Glue the undersides of the fern fronds to the brim of the hat.*

Larkspur (*Consolida ambigua*)

Lupidium grosso

2 *Make up small bunches of lupidium fern and larkspur, using 4 or 5 heads of the larkspur to a bunch. Wire the stems neatly using reel wire. You will need about 7 bunches.*

3 *Arrange the bunches of larkspur and fern around the hat in even groupings. Make sure the stems of one bunch are hidden under the flower heads of the next bunch.*

Hydrangea macrophylla

Adiantum sp.

Peonies (*Paeonia lactiflora*)

Roses

4 Then add the green hydrangea florets. Add the peonies, roses, rose leaves (previously steamed flat), and fern fronds in clusters around the hat, as shown.

5 Even up the arrangement and fill any gaps with rose leaves, more fern fronds, and tiny florets of hydrangea. Do not worry too much about symmetry, but try to make the decoration look evenly filled, without gaps.

Herb Pot Arrangement

This little arrangement is quick and easy to create. It makes an ideal decoration for a small table, or for individual place-settings for a dinner party.

MATERIALS

Oasis

Small herb jar

Ribbon (with same finish on both sides) for bow

Broken larkspur heads for filling

FLOWERS

2 stems pale blue larkspur (*Consolida ambigua*)

5 sprigs golden rod (*Solidago canadensis*)

3 florets *Hydrangea arborescens* 'Annabelle'

4 sprigs *Achillea* 'Moonshine'

2 poppy seed heads (*Papaver rhoeas*)

7 pink and 3 blue cornflowers (*Centaurea cyanus*)

4 red miniature floribunda roses

1 yellow hybrid tea rose

SMALL ARRANGEMENTS make a perfect decoration for the table. The one shown here is made up of a collection of summer flowers, but you could just as easily use a few yellow and blue flowers for spring, or berries and seed heads in autumn. It is a simple bouquet in a glass jar – in this case, a re-used herb jar. Fill the jar with something bright to match the flowers you use in the arrangement (I keep a box of leftover or broken flowers for filling). In the herb jar I used broken larkspur heads, but any small flower heads will serve the purpose. Even dried pulses, such as lentils or peas, look attractive, and help to weight the jar a little. Ideally, the colours of the filling should harmonize with those in the arrangement.

In this little bouquet, I used a classic flower arranger's shape, with the tallest flowers at the back, fanning out slightly towards the base. You should be careful not to make the arrangement too heavy or too tall for the jar. It will look unbalanced, and the jar could tip over.

The bow that provides the finishing touch should pick up one of the colours used in the arrangement. When you are using a wide palette of colours, as here, the ribbon helps to pull the arrangement together.

Standing no more than about 6 in (15 cm) high, this little herb pot is simple but effective. You can use any leftover flowers that you have in your cupboard; it helps to pull the colours together with a matching ribbon.

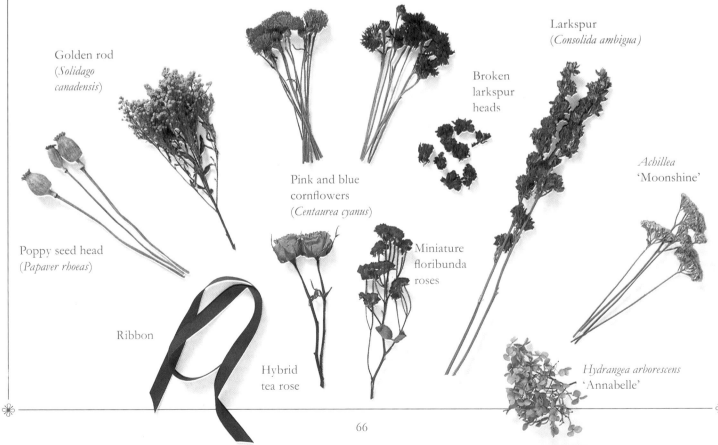

Golden rod (*Solidago canadensis*)

Broken larkspur heads

Larkspur (*Consolida ambigua*)

Achillea 'Moonshine'

Pink and blue cornflowers (*Centaurea cyanus*)

Poppy seed head (*Papaver rhoeas*)

Miniature floribunda roses

Ribbon

Hybrid tea rose

Hydrangea arborescens 'Annabelle'

Creating the arrangement

1 Break the flowers you are using to fill the jar into small florets and press them down well into the jar. Make a small plug of oasis for the neck of the jar, and press it in firmly.

2 Position the flowers which make the tallest and widest part of the arrangement. In this case, the larkspur provides height and the golden rod and hydrangea florets the width.

3 Start to fill out the arrangement with achillea, poppy seed heads, pink and blue cornflowers, and the miniature red roses, balancing the colours. Try to make sure that no light shines through.

4 Steam open the yellow rose (see page 58) and add it to the arrangement. Check that the shape is balanced. Then tie the ribbon around the neck of the jar.

Pair of Lavender Pots

Lavender grown in the garden derives its effect from large massed clumps, often formally clipped. The same principle is applied in this pair of simple-to-make pots.

MATERIALS

Paper ribbon
Clay pot 3 in (8 cm) in diameter
Oasis
Fine-gauge rose wire

FLOWERS

3–4 bunches lavender (*Lavandula angustifolia* 'Hidcote')

L AVENDER IS A great favourite of mine. It smells wonderful and it keeps its colour well when dried. I grow lots of it in the garden. Used on its own, as in this pair of formal pots, it has a strong sculptural form. The best type of lavender to use is a long-stemmed, dark blue form such as *Lavandula angustifolia* 'Hidcote'.

The secret of the success is to get the height of the lavender, the size of the pot, and the size of the bow in the proportions shown overleaf. If the pot is too big, the bow too small, or the lavender stems too tall or too short, the impact is lost. Because the pots are relatively small, standing about 12 in (30 cm) high, they look better in pairs. I like to put them on my kitchen dresser with my blue and white china or at each end of the mantelpiece, but they also look good on a dressing table.

When making the arrangement, it is important to use straight, well-formed heads of lavender. Discard any with bent stems or misshapen heads, but don't throw away the broken bits of lavender. You can keep them for later use in potpourri or to make lavender bags.

Overleaf: A pair of lavender pots sits on my kitchen dresser, surrounded by a collection of blue and white china. When making a pair, it will help if you make all the bunches for both pots at the same time to ensure that you get both arrangements the same height. Using matching paper ribbon for the bow is a key element in the design, which gains its impact from its simplicity. Make sure that the lavender is densely packed – don't be tempted to economize on the bunches.

Paper ribbon

Lavender (*Lavandula angustifolia* 'Hidcote')

Clay pot

Creating the arrangement

1 To cut the oasis to fit the inside of the clay pot, turn the pot upside down on the oasis, and press down firmly. The rim will leave a circular impression as a guideline.

2 Trim the oasis with a very sharp knife, gradually reducing it in size until it just fits the pot.

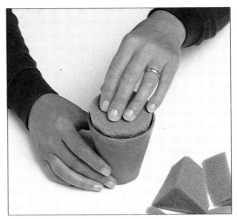

3 Insert the oasis into the pot, pressing down firmly. Trim if necessary to make sure that it fits snugly. The top of the oasis should be flush with the rim of the pot.

4 Make up small bunches (6 or 7 heads) of lavender. Make sure the heads are level by gently tapping them upside down on the table.

5 Bind the stems just below the heads with rose wire. Trim the ends of the stems with scissors to make bunches that are roughly 7 in (18 cm) in length.

6 Insert the bunches into the oasis, pressing down firmly. Make a dense arrangement of lavender heads with a conical shape that follows the lines of the clay pot.

7 Once the pot is almost full, go around the outside of the pot inserting small unwired bunches of lavender, slightly shorter than the others. This will hide the wires used to secure the other bunches, and produce a slightly domed effect.

8 Spread out the paper ribbon, tie it around the pot, and make a neat bow. Trim the ends to clear the base of the pot.

9 Even up any untidy heads by trimming the top of the arrangement lightly with a pair of scissors for a neat overall effect.

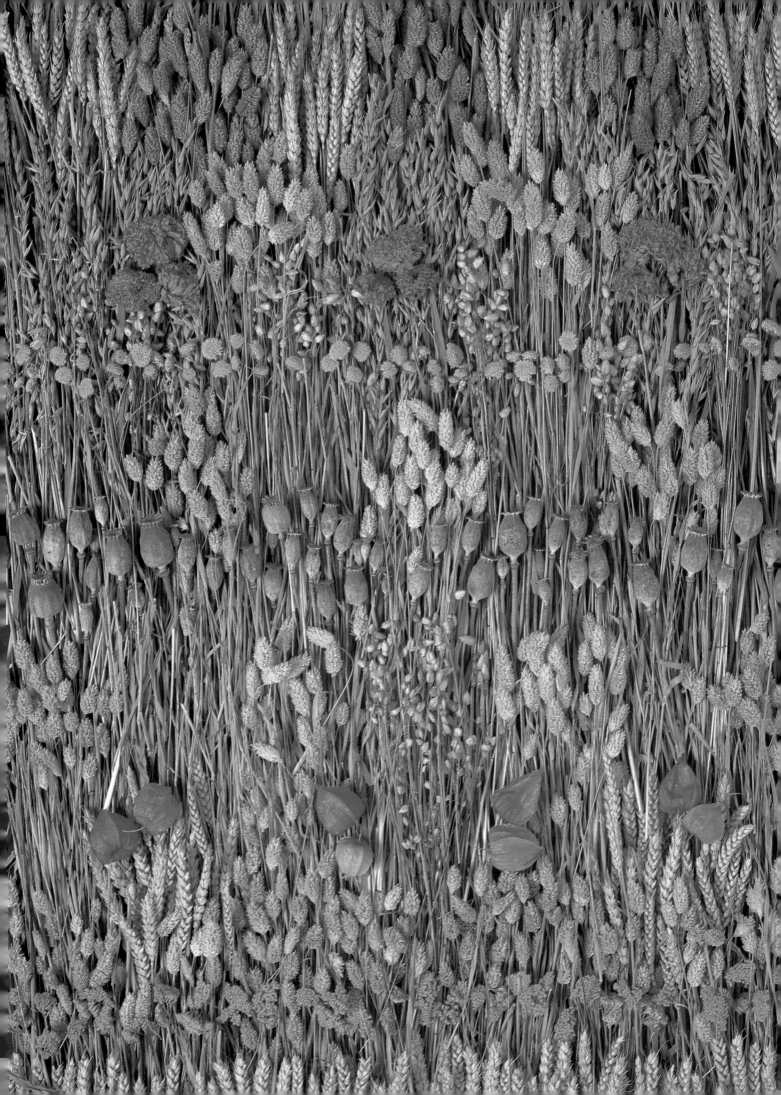

AUTUMN

If you happen to enjoy texture and form as much as colour, then autumn offers many opportunities for creating unusual arrangements.

WITH ITS RICH HARVEST of wheat and corn, and a wide range of seed heads, fruits and cones, autumn offers one of the most satisfying seasons for any dried flower arranger. The seed heads of so many plants, including poppies, alliums, and globe artichokes, make wonderful architectural shapes that are irresistible.

There are some late-flowering perennials that you can pick at this time of year, particularly small pom-pom dahlias and hydrangea heads, and many of the helichrysums in rich, warm colours. Golds, reds, and oranges seem to epitomize the best qualities of autumn, with its golden light and ripe harvest of garden produce.

Wild grasses and various forms of corn are also popular subjects for dried flower arrangements, and again there is a marvellous variety of shapes and colours. Some of my favourites include oats (*Avena sativa*), wheat (*Triticum aestivum*), and quaking grass (*Briza maxima*), and I tend to use them in architecturally shaped arrangements, sometimes softened with roses and marjoram or lavender.

Autumn is the time to start planting bulbs for the following spring, and I always make sure that I have plenty of the big *Allium christophii* in the garden, because their seed heads, used on their own, make spectacular dried flower arrangements.

One of my great delights in making autumn arrangements is to find appropriate non-plant material to enhance any dried flowers I have. The items that I think blend so well with autumn colours include clay pots and small baskets, bundles of pasta, peppercorns, and even plastic berries, provided they are in soft shades. Other objects that seem to go well with the autumn seed heads and grasses are small items of kitchen equipment and other garden produce – little metal pastry cutters in interesting shapes, miniature loaves of bread and heads of garlic, to name but a few. Look for interesting shapes in junk shops, and never throw out old kitchen equipment without first considering whether you can recycle it in your arrangements!

Autumn Flowers

Russet, bronze, gold, and orange are just some of the colours we associate with autumn. Here are some of my favourite dried autumn flowers.

Sea moss
(*Chenopodium aristatum*)

Hydrangea
(*Hydrangea arborescens* 'Annabelle')

Giant maidenhair fern
(*Adiantum formosum*)

Hydrangea
(*Hydrangea macrophylla*)

Hydrangea
(*Hydrangea macrophylla*)

Sea holly
(*Eryngium* sp.)

African marigold
(*Tagetes erecta*)

Dahlia
(*Dahlia* × *hortensis*)

Dahlia
(*Dahlia* × *hortensis*)

Dahlia
(*Dahlia* × *hortensis*)

Dahlia (*Dahlia × hortensis*)

Sea lavender
(*Goniolimon tartaricum*)

Lepidium ruderale

Large-flowered statice
(*Limonium latifolium*)

Eucalyptus sp., buds

Chinese lantern
(*Physalis alkekengi*)

China aster
(*Callistephus chinensis*)

Globe thistle
(*Echinops ritro*)

Knapweed
(*Centaurea macrocephala*)

Golden rod
(*Solidago canadensis*)

Strawflower
(*Helichrysum bracteatum*)

Grasses and seed heads seem to capture the spirit of autumn. Those shown here are a selection of some of the ones I often use. The small exotic seed heads and nuts that I use for texture in my arrangements are shown on pages 10–11.

Quaking grass
(*Briza maxima*)

Canary grass
(*Phalaris
canariensis*)

Canary grass
(*Phalaris canariensis*), dyed

Mint (*Mentha × piperita*
'Crispa') seedheads

Poppy seed heads
(*Papaver somniferum*)

Wheat
(*Triticum aestivum*)

Flax (*Linum usitatissimus*)

Bearded wheat
(*Triticale* sp.)

Caustus dioica

Love-in-a-mist
(*Nigella damascena*)
seed heads

*Nigella
orientalis*
seed heads

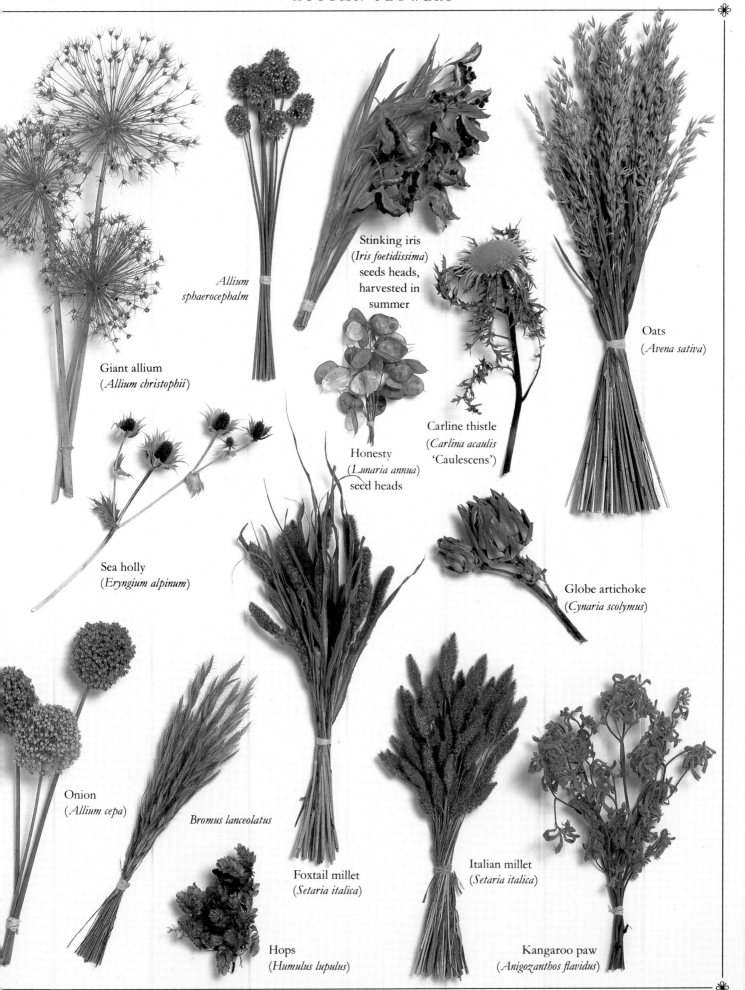

Giant allium
(*Allium christophii*)

*Allium
sphaerocephalm*

Stinking iris
(*Iris foetidissima*)
seeds heads,
harvested in
summer

Carline thistle
(*Carlina acaulis*
'Caulescens')

Oats
(*Avena sativa*)

Honesty
(*Lunaria annua*)
seed heads

Sea holly
(*Eryngium alpinum*)

Globe artichoke
(*Cynaria scolymus*)

Onion
(*Allium cepa*)

Bromus lanceolatus

Foxtail millet
(*Setaria italica*)

Italian millet
(*Setaria italica*)

Hops
(*Humulus lupulus*)

Kangaroo paw
(*Anigozanthos flavidus*)

Wheatsheaf

This arrangement requires no embellishment, and the shape of the arrangement is completely in harmony with the nature of the wheat itself.

MATERIALS

Oasis ball about 3½ in (8 cm) in diameter

Plastic flower pot 4½ in (12 cm) in diameter

3 garden canes 13 in (32 cm) long

Medium-gauge stub wire

Reel wire

FLOWERS

12 bunches wheat (*Triticum aestivum*)

WHEN I WAS A CHILD, all the cornfields were full of stooks of wheat at harvest time, and this striking arrangement is inspired by these memories. An ideal decoration for a church at harvest time, it also looks good standing in an alcove or in the hearth.

Although this arrangement looks simple, it does take time to make, and it is not particularly easy. Its appearance is deceptive in another way as well – the ears of wheat are not attached to the long stems. The arrangement is made in two distinct stages: first, the base of the sheaf is made using the stems, and then the spherical ball of wheat ears is constructed.

Check it frequently as you work on it to make sure that it is level and that the stems are evenly distributed. It is vital that the overall arrangement looks properly balanced, and this in turn depends on the size of the ball of wheat ears in relation to the length of the skirt. I normally use a ratio of about one-third (the depth of the head) to two-thirds (the depth of the skirt).

Because the structure is not simple to make, I experimented with various methods, and the one illustrated here works well. The structure on which the wheatsheaf is built must be stable and secure, so make sure that it is firmly wired.

As you work on the arrangement, try to achieve a nicely balanced conical shape, neither too spread out at the base nor too narrow.

A pair of these wheatsheaves look splendid positioned on either side of a fireplace, but the arrangement also looks good on its own in an alcove, as shown here.

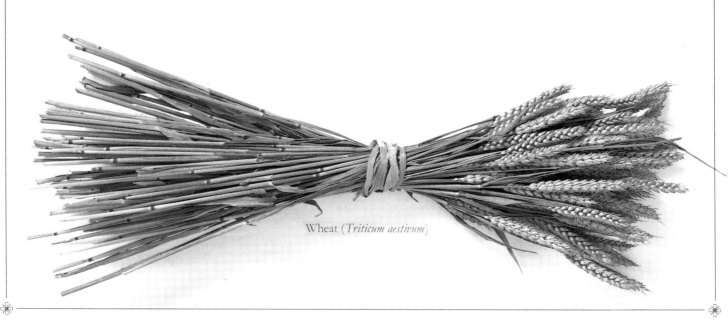

Wheat (*Triticum aestivum*)

Creating the arrangement

1 Insert the canes through the holes in the base of the pot. Wire the canes together at the head to form a wigwam shape, and wire each cane to the pot to create a firm base. Trim the canes level.

2 Take 6 to 7 wheat ears and trim the stems, leaving $1\frac{1}{2}$ in (4 cm) of stalk. Wire them directly under the wheat ears, leaving a short tail of wire. Take 6 to 7 stems, strip off leaves and wire thinner ends together, leaving a short tail.

3 Push the oasis ball firmly down on to the top of the canes, about 1 in (2.5 cm) deep, until it is firmly anchored.

4 Take the bunches of stems made in step 2. Measure the length against the structure before you trim the stems level, leaving an extra 1 in (2.5 cm) for inserting into the oasis ball.

5 Insert the bunches of stems into the base of the oasis ball, working around it to create the skirt.

6 Holding the stems with one hand, trim so that they are the same length as the underlying structure.

7 Bind the top of the skirt with reel wire, about 4 in (10 cm) below the oasis ball. Thread the wire in and out of the stems, and twist to fasten.

8 Make the ball part of the arrangement by pushing the stalks of the bunches of wheat ears into the oasis, starting at the bottom.

9 Continue working around the oasis ball, pushing the bunches well into the oasis. Make sure that they are evenly distributed in a globe shape.

10 Trim the base again if necessary so that the arrangement stands firm and square, and trim any whiskers off the wheat ears.

Shelf Arrangement

Bands of colour – in pinks, mauves, greens, blues, and yellows – make up this arrangement. I used larkspur, celosia, roses, marjoram, caustus, and golden rod, but you can copy the idea using whatever dried flowers are available, provided the colours and shapes work well together.

MATERIALS

Basket about 9 in (24 cm) long by 4 in (10 cm) wide
Oasis

FLOWERS

1 bunch larkspur (*Consolida ambigua*)
2 bunches *Celosia argentea cristata*
1½ bunches marjoram (*Origanum vulgare*)
2 bunches small-flowered pink roses
1 bunch *Caustus* sp.
1 bunch golden rod (*Solidago canadensis*)

THE IDEA IS TO CREATE gently contrasting bands of colour in a stepped effect. Once you understand the basic concept – which is to produce an arrangement of co-ordinating hues – you can apply it to any arrangement, varying the colours and size of the flowers.

As discussed in the introduction, it is very important to understand the effect that colours have on each other. For example, a layer of white flowers in the centre would effectively have cut the arrangement in half.

The proportions of the arrangement also influence the overall effect. If the structure is too tall and thin, it looks mean; if it is too short and squat, it lacks elegance. Remember that the arrangement will also be seen in profile, so do not neglect the sides.

Overleaf: The container you choose for this arrangement is very important because it makes, in effect, a third band of colour. I think the rush-covered container here is very successful.

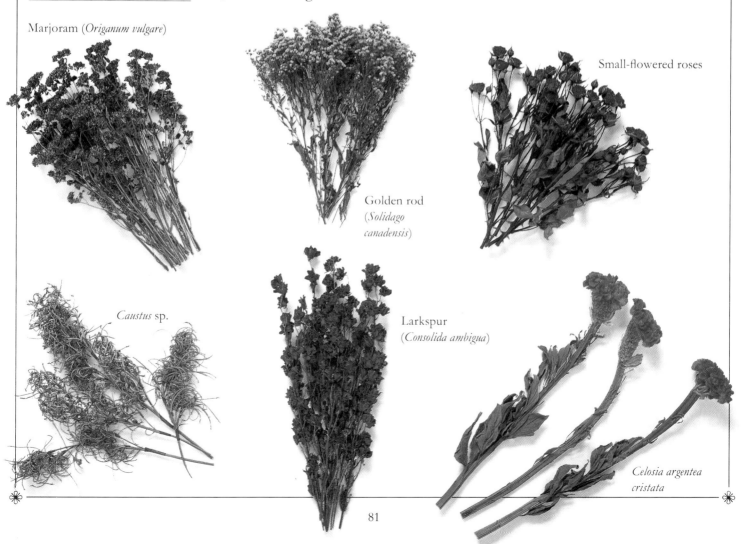

Marjoram (*Origanum vulgare*)

Small-flowered roses

Golden rod (*Solidago canadensis*)

Caustus sp.

Larkspur (*Consolida ambigua*)

Celosia argentea cristata

Creating the arrangement

1 Insert a block of oasis into the basket, at least 2 in (5 cm) higher than the basket rim. Insert the larkspur at the back.

2 Insert the celosia in front of the larkspur. To create a stepped effect, make some stems shorter than others.

3 Insert the marjoram in front of the celosia in the same way, fanning the flowers slightly at the sides.

4 Cut the thorns off the rose stems – it is easier to insert them into the oasis if they are smooth – and insert them in front of and below the marjoram, again stepping the heads.

5 At this stage, check that the arrangement is balanced, fanning out any stems at the sides of the arrangement so that it is wider at the top than at the bottom.

6 Insert the caustus (shortening the stems and stripping off small heads if necessary), both in front of the roses and at the sides of the arrangement.

7 Insert sprigs of the golden rod in any gaps at the front and sides of the arrangement to add bright colour at the base. Cover any exposed oasis at the back with remaining sprigs of golden rod.

Harvest Swag

This elegant pair of swags makes good use of harvest-time produce such as wheat, cones, and seed heads and the soft autumn shades of gold, russet, and brown.

FLOWERS

6 bunches wheat (*Triticum aestivum*)
4 bunches oregano (*Oreganum dictamnus*)
3 bunches *Hydrangea arborescens* 'Annabelle' florets
5 bunches dahlias
4 bunches pink peppercorns
4 larch cones (*Larix* sp.)
4 pine cones (*Pinus* sp.)
4 large and 4 small lotus seed heads
1 bunch oats (*Avena sativa*)

A UTUMN-FLOWERING PLANTS make particularly good subjects for swags and wreaths, as the seed heads and cones make strong shapes in their own right. I like to emphasize these with the use of sculptural objects such as baskets and pots, which echo the shape and texture of fruits and seeds. For contrasting texture I use oats and wheat, with a few softer elements like hydrangea heads and dahlias to "lift" the swag and give it more life.

The soft browns, pinks, and golds of this particular swag make it ideally suited to hang over a fireplace with an open fire, the colours echoing the warmth of the hearth. Although I like to hang swags in pairs, you could just as easily have only one.

If you are making a pair, do not worry if they are not symmetrical. You have to adjust them anyway once they are hanging, and minor differences between the two are part of the charm. The main aim is to ensure that the overall impact is balanced. You may find your swag benefits from a bunch or two extra of one particular flower, and fewer of another.

MATERIALS ·

1-in (3-cm) chicken wire, 28 in (70 cm) long × 8 in (20 cm) wide
Sphagnum moss
Medium-gauge stub wire
3 baskets
3 small clay pots
Paper ribbon

The swag on the left of the picture is shown in the step-by-step photographs that follow. If it looks a bit different that's because I had to make a few adjustments when it was hanging, as I discovered that I had made its twin rather fatter!

Securing the hook

Dried flower arrangements that are to be hung up need to be worked on while they are hanging, so that you can check for any gaps or holes that are visible from below. You can make a simple hook with florist's wire.

1 *After the base has been made, insert a 9-in (23-cm) length of medium-gauge stub wire through the back, weaving it through both sides of one of the squares of chicken wire.*

2 *Twist the ends of the wire over each other, then twist one end down over one side of the loop. Repeat with the other end and make a neat loop with no sharp ends.*

Creating the arrangement

1 Cut the chicken wire to the required width and length, and lay it flat on the table. Place the moss down the centre of the wire thick enough to form a solid base and distribute it evenly along the length.

2 Grasp both sides of the chicken wire and hook the two sides together to form a sausage shape. Fold over any cut wires to make sure there are no sharp edges.

Wheat
(*Triticum aestivum*)

Paper ribbon

Pine cone
(*Pinus* sp.)

Larch cones
(*Larix* sp.)

Clay pot

3 Turn the swag base over, so that the join is underneath. Make six wired bundles of wheat (see page 80). Arrange on the swag to form three diagonal crosses.

4 Add the pots (see page 121 for wiring instructions) as shown, facing in opposite directions. Wire the baskets by pushing the wire through the side of the basket and fastening them to the swag.

5 Add bunches of oregano in pairs on either side of the wreath. Keep the heads upright, and place a final bunch across the base of the wreath to cover the end.

Peppercorns

Oregano
(*Oreganum dictamnus*)

Oats (*Avena sativa*)

Hydrangea arborescens 'Annabelle'

Dahlias

Lotus seed heads
(large and small)

Basket

Flat moss

6 Add the hydrangea florets and the dahlias, then the peppercorns, lotus seed heads, and cones. Use the glue gun (see page 120) for delicate flowers and seed heads. There is no hard and fast rule about where to place the different elements; just aim for a contrast in shape, colour, and texture.

7 Insert small cones or bunches of peppercorns in the baskets, using the glue gun. Make up a large bunch of oats with a paper ribbon bow, and attach it to the top of the swag.

Architectural Arrangement with Roses

I have this arrangement on a desk at home, and it always attracts favourable comments. The combination of the stiff stems of wheat with the softness of the roses and marjoram works very well.

MATERIALS

Rush basket about 8 in (20 cm) square

Oasis

Reel wire

FLOWERS

4 big bunches of wheat (*Triticum aestivum*)

3 bunches of marjoram (*Origanum vulgare*)

2 bunches (40 stems) of pink-red roses

W HEAT LOOKS BEST when used in solid blocks, rather than added in single stems. In my arrangements, I always use it in bunches, as in the Harvest swag (page 84), or in blocks, as in the Wheatsheaf (page 78), or as here, where I have softened it with roses and marjoram.

Although all dried flower arrangements fade in time, this one looks, if anything, even more attractive as the colours soften and blend.

When you are making it, be patient and make fairly small bunches of wheat. If you try to hurry and push large bunches into the block of oasis, it will simply break up. When you are working, try to be as neat as possible. The ears of wheat must look straight and even.

The arrangement is quite tall – about 18 in (45 cm) high – and needs to be seen on its own, rather than surrounded with objects. It would be ideal for a hall table.

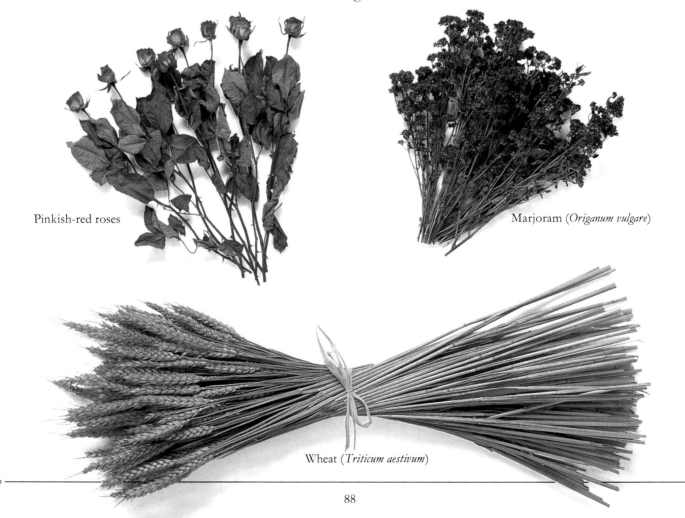

Pinkish-red roses

Marjoram (*Origanum vulgare*)

Wheat (*Triticum aestivum*)

Creating the arrangement

1 Fill the basket tightly with blocks of oasis deep enough to make a solid base.

2 Bunch together about 6 to 8 ears of wheat and wire them near the base. Make sure the bunches are an even length – about 18 in (45 cm).

3 Start to fill the basket with rows of wheat bunches, leaving a ½ in (1.5 cm) margin around the edge of the basket.

4 Continue adding the bunches of wheat, making sure that you leave no space between the heads.

5 Fill the basket, leaving ½ in (1.5 cm) space around the edges. Insert single stems of wheat around the outside to disguise the wired parts.

6 Add the marjoram around the outside, with the shortest stems at the corners.

7 Add the roses in a stepped effect around each side of the arrangement. Roses in each row should alternate so that no rose is directly above or below another.

8 Check for any gaps, and fill with some of the rose leaves if necessary. Make sure the marjoram rises to a definable point at the centre of each side.

Decorated Basket

This is one of the larger and more time-consuming projects. Once you have mastered the technique of making the rope of hay to go around the basket edge it is not particularly difficult.

FLOWERS

2 bunches *Eucalyptus* sp., dyed blue
2 bunches marjoram (*Origanum vulgare*)
2 bunches love-lies-bleeding (*Amaranthus* sp.)
2 bunches lavender (*Lavandula angustifolia* 'Hidcote')
1 bunch *Alchemilla mollis*
2 bunches poppy seed heads (*Papaver somniferum*)
6 small bunches pink and red plastic berries
5 larch cones (*Larix* sp.)
2 lotus seed heads (*Nelumbo lucifera*)
10 peonies (*Paeonia lactiflora*)
Potpourri (see page 123)

THIS ARRANGEMENT is one of my favourites. It is rich in colour, has a wonderful scent, and can be used in almost any room of the house. It sums up what I most enjoy about dried flowers – their delicacy, their scent, and their richness.

I particularly like the contrasts in texture (the softness of the potpourri petals against the hardness of the basket), the deep tones of the peonies, and the generous nature of the arrangement. Incorporating cones and seed heads in the arrangement creates an attractive textural effect.

Dried flowers are quite expensive, but you can save money by drying flowers from your own garden (see page 17). You will probably still have to buy the more exotic flowers from a florist's shop, but fillers and greenery can often be successfully dried at home.

Make your own potpourri to go in the centre of this arrangement (see page 123). Use broken flower heads or half-bunches left over from other arrangements, but do not fill the entire basket with potpourri. Cover the base with crumpled tissue paper, put some dry moss on top, then cover with a layer of potpourri.

MATERIALS

Basket with handle, 12 in (30 cm) in diameter
Bag of hay (obtainable from a pet shop)
Florist's medium-gauge stub wire
Dried flat moss

Overleaf: Decorating the rim of a wicker basket with dried flowers and filling it with potpourri creates a deliciously scented table centre.

Poppy seed heads (*Papaver somniferum*)

Lavender (*Lavandula angustifolia* 'Hidcote')

Love-lies-bleeding (*Amaranthus* sp.)

Alchemilla mollis

Lotus seed head (*Nelumbo lucifera*)

Eucalyptus sp.

Larch cones (*Larix* sp.)

Peonies (*Paeonia lactiflora*)

Marjoram (*Origanum vulgare*)

Potpourri

Plastic berries

Creating the arrangement

1 Cover the basket edge with a rope of hay (see page 119). Space 10 bunches of eucalyptus, with 5 sprigs per bunch, equally around the basket, leaving a tail of wire.

2 Make up 10 small bunches of marjoram. Wire them to the hay rope, facing in the same direction as the eucalyptus. Cover the stems of the eucalyptus each time.

3 Make up 6 small bunches of lavender and 6 of red amaranthus. Wire them to the hay rope in the same direction as the previous flowers.

4 Make up 4 bunches of alchemilla, with 4 stems to a bunch. Insert them in the same direction as the other flowers, but position them so that they help to fill the inside edge of the rim.

5 Make up 5 bunches of poppy seed heads with 5 heads in each bunch, and insert them crosswise to create a contrast of shape.

6 Use the plastic berries next – 3 bunches of red ones, and 3 of pink – to create a similar contrast in shape.

7 Add the 5 larch cones and the 2 lotus seed heads wherever needed in the arrangement to create a contrast of texture. (See pages 121–2 for wiring techniques.)

8 For the final decoration, trim the stalks off 10 peonies and steam open if necessary (see page 58). Glue the underside of the flower heads to the arrangement.

9 Fill the basket two-thirds to the brim with dark fabric or tissue paper. Cover this with a layer of dried moss, then a top layer of potpourri. Add a few silica-gel-dried flowers.

Tapestry of Flowers

The shape of the container and the neatly blocked triangles of contrasting colours give this arrangement the appearance of a needlepoint hassock.

MATERIALS

Wicker basket 12 in (30 cm)
long × 10½ in (26 cm)
wide × 3 in (8 cm) deep

Oasis

Heavy-gauge stub wire

FLOWERS

40 mini poppy seed heads
(*Papaver rhoeas*)

4 African marigolds
(*Tagetes erecta*)

2 bunches *Ageratum* sp.

1 bunch everlasting
(*Helichrysum* sp.)

18 red carnations (*Dianthus* sp.)

Dyed green lichen moss

STRONG CONTRASTING COLOURS in neat horizontal blocks give this arrangement its impact. I have used marigolds, carnations, everlasting, and ageratum, with lichen moss to set them off, but you can choose your own flowers. Ideally, the heads should make a fairly dense mass when grouped together, so choose flowers that have their colour at the end of the stem, rather than along a spike. Roses would be ideal, as would achillea and peonies.

It is one of the easiest arrangements to construct: the only wires needed are those which section off the blocks of colour. Although I have chosen to divide this basket with diagonal rows of poppy heads, filling the spaces in between with colour, I have also made similar arrangements with the colours blocked into rows. If you wish, you could create a row all around the four sides of the basket, and then subsequent rows of colour within this, leaving a neat rectangle in the centre. Another possibility would be to repeat flowers in alternate rows.

This tapestry of flowers looks best seen from above, so that you get the full impact of the dense colours. Strong colour contrasts like this work well when they are kept simple and defined in blocked areas.

Making the base

Make sure that the top of the oasis is even. Use wire, as I have, or tape to create the guidelines for the design.

1 Fill the basket with oasis to within ¾ in (2 cm) of the rim. When the flowers are inserted, they should be level with the top of the basket or only slightly higher.

2 Divide the surface of the oasis into six sections. The easiest way to do this is to insert three lengths of stub wire as your guidelines. A strip of tape works well too.

Creating the arrangement

1 Following the lines of wire, create a framework for the arrangement with rows of poppy seed heads. Leave $\frac{1}{2}$ in (1.5 cm) of stalk above the oasis.

2 Steam open the marigold heads as shown in the instructions for steaming open roses on page 58. Insert them around the centre of the arrangement in a solid block of colour.

3 Insert the heads of ageratum; try to get them as level as possible. Make sure that you have inserted enough flowers to give an appropriately dense effect.

Carnations (*Dianthus* sp.)

African marigolds · (*Tagetes erecta*)

Everlasting (*Helichrysum* sp.)

4 Add the everlasting heads next in the 2 facing triangles. Steam open the carnation heads in the same manner as before (see page 58), and add them in the other 2 triangles.

5 Surround the gap between the flowers and the basket edge with a ribbon of moss. (It is easy to pull this type of moss apart and then roll it into a ribbon.) Use a stick or the end of a pen to push in the moss.

Mini poppy seed heads (*Papaver rhoeas*)

Lichen moss

Ageratum sp.

6 Pull the poppy heads up slightly – about $\frac{3}{4}$ in (2 cm) – so that they make a well-defined row in between each of the blocks of colour.

WINTER

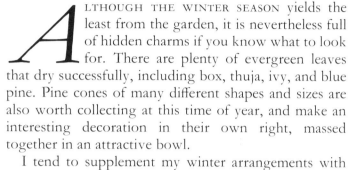

Rich, glossy green leaves, scarlet berries and sharp, spiky pine needles give winter arrangements a very special appearance, strong in both form and colour.

ALTHOUGH THE WINTER SEASON yields the least from the garden, it is nevertheless full of hidden charms if you know what to look for. There are plenty of evergreen leaves that dry successfully, including box, thuja, ivy, and blue pine. Pine cones of many different shapes and sizes are also worth collecting at this time of year, and make an interesting decoration in their own right, massed together in an attractive bowl.

I tend to supplement my winter arrangements with nuts and fruit, which have a seasonal appeal and offer some very satisfying shapes to work with. Kumquats, tangerines, and oranges are all in season, and dried fruit slices (see page 122) work well with most other ingredients. Chestnuts, walnuts, and hazelnuts, threaded into bracelets or grouped into a net, make a valuable addition to many dried flower arrangements. I also enjoy using thick white candles – they look particularly good surrounded by winter evergreens.

When using perishable ingredients in an arrangement, it is best to spray them first. Fruit slices, for example, will keep almost indefinitely if first coated on both sides with clear polyurethane varnish (available in hardware shops). To prevent mess when spraying, I always use a cardboard box, standing on its side. Put the item to be sprayed in the box, and then spray into the box itself.

Winter is a good time of year to find lichen, twigs, and moss. You often see twigs and foliage in flower shops that have been sprayed with red or gold paint to use in Christmas arrangements, and it is quite easy to do this yourself. You can spray poppy heads and cones with equal success.

Winter is also a good time to pick foliage for drying. Mahonia leaves can be picked and then dried between sheets of newspaper. I have special places in my house where I always use a dried arrangement because there is not sufficient light for fresh flowers. I pick small-leaved evergreens from the garden, such as box or hebe, and combine them with dried flowers to great effect. Sometimes I combine them with silk or parchment flowers, allowing the fresh greenery to dry naturally in the vase.

Winter Flowers

In the winter months, even though there are fewer flowers available, there's a wealth of good evergreen foliage, including the holiday favourites like box, ivy, and thuja, which can successfully be air dried.

Thuja placata

Eucalyptus sp.,
juvenile foliage, dyed

Spider gum
(*Eucalyptus* sp.)

Eucalyptus sp.,
juvenile foliage, dyed

Hebe rakaiensis

Roundleaf eucalyptus
(*Eucalyptus* sp.)

Blue pine (*Abies* sp.)

Tree ivy
(*Hedera helix*)

Oak (*Quercus robur*),
harvested in summer and dyed

Common holly
(*Ilex aquifolium*)

Variegated holly
(*Ilex aquifolium*), fresh

Box (*Buxus sempervirens*)

Heather
(*Erica* sp.)

Sphagnum moss
(*Pleurozium schreberi*)

Tillandsia sp.

Club moss
(*Retinospora* sp.)

Flat moss
(*Hypnum cupressiforme*)

Lichen moss
(*Cladonia* sp.), dyed

Bun moss
(*Leucobryum glaucum*)

Ivy (*Hedera* sp.),
dyed and glycerined

Christmas Table Centrepiece

Candlelight and a flickering fire seem to sum up the spirit of Christmas. This arrangement can be used as a dinner table decoration, or on its own, as here, on a low coffee table.

FLOWERS

Sphagnum moss
3 large pine cones (*Pinus* sp.)
4 bunches of lavender (*Lavandula angustifolia* 'Hidcote')
3 large oranges
3 wired clay pots (see page 121)
6 satsumas
5 pomegranates
Club moss
15 dried orange slices, in bunches of 3
6 picks of artificial cherries
Dyed green lichen moss
Hazelnuts

CHRISTMAS IS A wonderful opportunity to fill the house with flowers and foliage. Although I love traditional Christmas decorations, it is also good, for a change, to experiment with something seasonal but different.

This table centrepiece makes use of fruit as much as flowers and foliage, with oranges, satsumas, artificial cherries, nuts, and cones. It includes candles, too, which can be lit, provided you do not leave them unattended.

The container I have used is a humble cake tin, admittedly a very old one. I think its plainness sets off the elaborate construction above it and adds an almost Renaissance quality to the arrangement, reminding one of pewter plates at medieval banquets.

The lavender, cones, and oranges emit a delicate, spicy scent, particularly appropriate for this time of year.

MATERIALS

Round cake tin 10 in (25 cm) in diameter
4 wax candles 10 in (25 cm) tall
Heavy-gauge stub wire
Oasis
Medium-gauge stub wire
Adhesive tape

The spirit of Christmas! The fruit, fire, and candlelight create a warm glowing atmosphere.

Wiring candles

You can buy candle holders for standard-sized candles, but with the large ones such as these, each candle has to be wired individually so that it can be fixed firmly to the oasis.

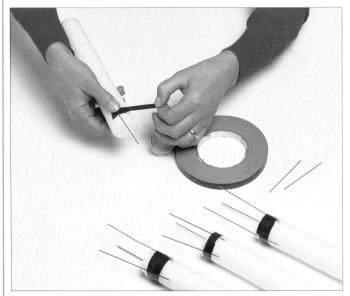

1 Cut three equal lengths of heavy-gauge wire about 4 in (10 cm) long. Holding the first piece of wire against the candle, bind it to the base of the candle with adhesive tape.

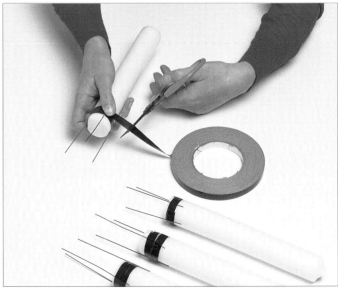

2 Carry on binding and wiring the base of the candle as shown. Repeat for each of the 4 candles. Make sure that all three wires for each candle are solidly fixed.

Sphagnum moss

Wax candle

Dyed green lichen moss

Lavender (*Lavandula angustifolia* 'Hidcote')

Large pine cone (*Pinus* sp.)

Clay pot

Hazelnuts

Orange

Artificial cherries

Satsumas

Pomegranate

Club moss

Dried orange slices

Creating the arrangement

1 Put a large block of oasis into the cake tin, with a half-block on top. Hold the top block in place with a hairpin-shaped piece of stub wire. Fill the space around the oasis with sphagnum moss if necessary.

2 Insert the wire candle-holders into the bottom block of oasis at the four corners, making sure that the candles are stable.

3 Drape a little sphagnum moss on the oasis around the base of each candle to disguise the oasis.

4 Wire the pine cones (see page 121). Insert them upright into the oasis between the candles.

5 Split each of the 4 big bunches of lavender in half, and wire just underneath the heads, leaving a tail of wire. Trim the stalks level at the base. Insert the bunches in crossed pairs into the 4 sides of the oasis.

6 Add the 3 large oranges and wired clay pots (see page 121), angled outwards, in the spaces between the candles, the cones, and the lavender. Wedge the oranges in place with a little sphagnum moss if necessary.

7 Add the satsumas (wired if necessary – see page 122), the pomegranates, and the club moss to build a slightly conical shape. If necessary, add more sphagnum moss to hold these in place.

8 Use the bunches of dried orange slices to cover the wiring of the crossed pairs of lavender and fill the spaces between the cones. Add the picks of cherries around the edges.

9 Partially fill the clay pots with lichen moss to hide the wiring, and add the hazelnuts to the pots. Fill any holes or gaps with moss.

Christmas Door Wreath

A Christmas door wreath should be welcoming, and I like to make mine both colourful and different.

DECORATION

30–35 small bunches blue pine (*Picea pungens glauca*)
4 bundles cinnamon sticks
2 tartan four-looped bows
2 *Sterculia* pods
6 larch cones (*Larix* sp.)
6 pine cones (*Pinus* sp.)
6 bunches variegated fresh holly (*Ilex* sp.)
4 limes
3 bunches dried orange slices
3 bunches kumquats
2 palm fronds, dried
6 lotus seed heads
2 bunches golden mushrooms
1 bunch chestnuts
10 walnuts
Brown paper ribbon

CHRISTMAS IS a wonderful time for experimenting with all kinds of seasonal arrangements, and these days I find myself using lots of Christmas produce – particularly different kinds of nuts and fruit.

Fresh fruit is fine to use in a Christmas arrangement that has to last only a couple of weeks. The decoration is taken down before the fruit begins to rot, but the dried fruit slices, being varnished, last indefinitely, as do the nuts. This kind of arrangement clearly benefits from the shelter of a porch, but varnishing any fruit used helps to make the wreath more weatherproof.

It is important to make sure that the base is solid and firm, because the ingredients to be attached are quite heavy. Do not skimp on these ingredients; nothing looks worse than a few sparse decorations attached to a large base. Even if you choose different ingredients, it is essential that the wreath base is fully covered with blue pine, and that this in turn is well covered.

MATERIALS

Wreath base 14 in (35 cm) in diameter
Sphagnum moss
Mossing wire
Medium-gauge stub wire
Green garden string

The Christmas door wreath, like any wreath hung on a door which is opened and shut frequently, needs to be made quite carefully. Attach the decorations securely, or they will fall off every time the door is slammed!

Making the base

You can use a ready-made wreath base (available from a good florist's store) or make your own out of thick garden wire or a couple of wire coat hangers bent into a circle.

1 *Wedge the moss around the base of the ring and wire it in place by winding the mossing wire over and over the wreath. Mark the starting point with scissors.*

2 *Continue to wind the wire around the wreath base. Make a loop for hanging the wreath at the back of the base (see page 84).*

3 *Wire together 3 sprigs of blue pine for each bunch, leaving a short tail of stub wire. Bind loosely to the wreath with string, the heads overlapping the stems.*

Creating the arrangement

1 Make 4 bundles of cinnamon sticks, binding each bundle with an elastic band. Wire crossed pairs of cinnamon sticks to opposite sides of the wreath.

2 Add the tartan bows to the centre of each of the crossed pairs of cinnamon sticks. The bows will serve to hide the elastic bands and wire.

3 Add the sterculia pods and the larch and pine cones, bunched together with 3 of each to a bunch. Instructions for wiring are given on page 121.

4 Make 6 bunches of holly, 3 sprigs to a bunch, and add them to the outer edges of the wreath at carefully spaced intervals to balance the shape.

5 Add the limes (wired as shown on page 122) and arrange them to pick up the colour of the holly. Add the dried orange slices (see page 122) as shown.

6 Add the kumquats in bunches, 3 to a bunch, and add the dried palm fronds in any suitable spaces in the arrangement, trying to balance the shape.

Palm frond

Variegated fresh holly
(*Ilex* sp.)

Golden mushrooms

Cinnamon sticks

Larch cones
(*Larix* sp.)

Sterculia pod

Tartan four-looped bows

Dried orange slices

Pine cone (*Pinus* sp.)

Lotus seed heads

Lime

Kumquats

Blue pine
(*Picea pungens glauca*)

Brown paper
ribbon

Walnuts

Chestnuts

7 Check the wreath from the side, and fill in any gaps with cones and lotus seed heads. Add the golden mushrooms.

8 Add the chestnuts, in groups of 4 to 5 (see page 121), and add the walnuts singly to fill in any gaps.

9 Make a large bow from paper ribbon (see page 124) and fix in place at the base of the wreath.

Christmas Garland

*Make a Christmas garland for the staircase, as I have done. Garlands also look
lovely over a door frame or mantelpiece, if you prefer to create something less elaborate.*

DECORATION

10 large pine cones (*Pinus* sp.)
5 bunches lavender (*Lavandula angustifolia* 'Hidcote')
5 clay pots
3 bundles cinnamon sticks (5/6 sticks to a bundle)
5 bunches dried orange slices (4 slices to a bunch)
6 orange ribbon bows
3 bunches almonds, held in hairnets
5 biscuits, tied with raffia
5 pink paper ribbon bows
1 bunch *Artemisia* sp.

FOR THIS GARLAND, I used a varied selection of decorations – clay pots, cinnamon sticks, and biscuits for texture; orange slices, lavender, and bows for colour.

The cheapest and easiest base for the garland is black plastic bin liners, cut down each side so that they open out into a long rectangle. These are then covered with bunches of blue pine. You could use other garden evergreens instead, but they may dry out quickly.

You can attach whatever takes your fancy to the garland, although do be careful. The biscuits I used proved irresistible to a visiting friend's Labrador dog!

Because the garland loops up the banisters, you have to decide where to attach the decorations. Try to space fairly evenly, but avoid trying to be too symmetrical, as the winding base will make it difficult to be consistent.

MATERIALS
(for the base – 9 ft (3 m) in length)

Black plastic bin liners
Mossing wire
Blue pine (*Picea pungens glauca*)
Green garden string
Medium-gauge stub wire

The staircase garland seen from below. Ideally, it should look colourful and full, but not too heavily decorated. The aim is to allow enough of the blue pine base to be seen to add to the festive effect.

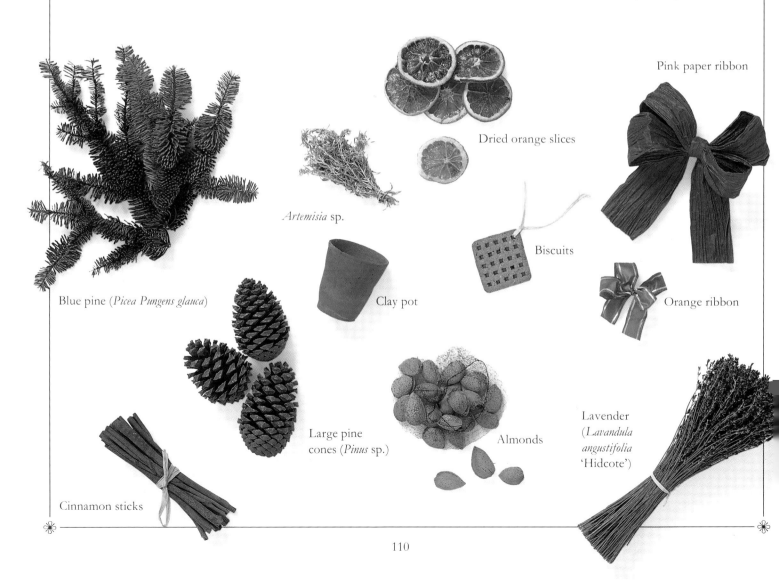

Dried orange slices

Artemisia sp.

Pink paper ribbon

Biscuits

Clay pot

Orange ribbon

Blue pine (*Picea Pungens glauca*)

Large pine cones (*Pinus* sp.)

Almonds

Lavender (*Lavandula angustifolia* 'Hidcote')

Cinnamon sticks

Creating the arrangement

1 *Cut the black plastic bin liners down both sides to make a rectangle. Secure the ends of the black plastic rectangle with mossing wire, but do not cut the wire.*

2 *Take a bunch of blue pine and lay it with the head covering the end of the liner. Bind it into place with the mossing wire. Add the next bunch with the head over the stem of the first.*

3 *When all the blue pine sprigs are secured to the base, bind them loosely with green garden string. This will stop the garland from opening out when it is looped up and fastened to the banisters.*

4 Fasten the garland base to the banisters with wire, making sure it is looped evenly. Add the cones in groups, wired as shown on page 121.

5 Add the bunches of lavender, held together with elastic bands and bound with raffia to conceal the bands.

6 Fasten the clay pots to the garland, wired with two stub wires per pot as shown on page 121.

7 Add the bundles of cinnamon sticks, fastened with elastic bands and neatly tied around the centre of each bundle with raffia to hide the bands.

8 Add the dried orange slices, which should be varnished and wired in bunches of 4 (see page 122).

9 Add the bows (see page 124 for instructions on how to tie) near the orange slices to pick up the colour.

10 Tie about 15 almonds into a hairnet, or similar very fine netting, and attach to the garland base with wire.

11 Add the biscuits, tied with raffia. (Biscuits with a hole, or holes, can be attached easily.)

12 Finally, fill the clay pots with sprigs of artemisia to hide the wires which hold the pots in place.

Christmas Tree

*Green and red – echoing the leaves and berries of holly – are the traditional colours
for Christmas decorations, shown off to great effect in this elegant little table decoration.*

MATERIALS

Clay pot
Plaster of Paris
Stout garden stick about 10 in (25 cm) long
1 in (2.5 cm) nail
1 in (2.5 cm) gauge chicken wire
Fine-gauge stub wire

DECORATION

Sprigs of blue pine (*Picea pungens glauca*), approximately 2 branches
20 bunches red plastic berries
25–30 pasta bows, wired

CHRISTMAS DECORATIONS can be expensive, but this little tree, made from blue pine and decorated with scarlet pasta bows and red berries, makes an attractive table decoration with the added advantage that it costs very little. Blue pine is normally plentiful around Christmas, and you can use leftover pieces from a garland, for example, for this project. It is important, though, to use only the tips of the pine. Make sure that you have enough to cover the structure properly, for it will not look attractive if you skimp on it.

Make the pasta bows in advance; simply spray uncooked pasta shapes with car paint. I normally do this by arranging the bows on oasis in a box, and then spraying into it. Spray one side of the bows, let them dry, then spray the other side. Spraying the finished bows with gloss polyurethane gives added shine.

The frame of the tree needs to be set in plaster of Paris so that it is firmly weighted, as you have to exert considerable pressure when pushing the sprigs of blue pine into the sub-frame. A good stout stick from the garden will serve as the trunk for the tree. To create the frame for the pine, hammer a large nail into the top of the stick and use doubled-over chicken wire to form a pyramid shape. Attach the chicken wire to the nail with a piece of stub wire.

Barely 12 in (30 cm) tall, this elegant small Christmas tree would make a table decoration or even a substitute for a larger tree in a small flat.

Red plastic berries

Blue pine (*Picea pungens glauca*)

Pasta bows

Creating the arrangement

1 Hammer a nail into the centre of a stick set in plaster of Paris (see page 50).

2 Bend doubled-over chicken wire into a cone and squeeze the edges together. Wire it to the nail.

3 Add small sprigs of blue pine to the base of the structure, making sure the ends are firmly secured in the chicken wire. Insert them at right angles to the pot.

4 Continue adding the blue pine from the base upwards, creating a Christmas tree shape. Stop about 3 in (7.5 cm) from the top of the tree.

5 Now add the blue pine from the top downwards, using smaller tips of pine. The pine should slope down attractively to make a suitably pointed shape.

6 Add the red plastic berries, arranging them evenly over the tree, and push the wires into the blue pine in order to secure them firmly in place.

7 Wire the pasta bows around the centre of each bow, leaving tails long enough to go through the pine and catch on the chicken wire. Push them into the blue pine in the spaces between the berries.

Techniques

THE TECHNIQUES for creating professional-looking dried flower arrangements are relatively few and easily learned. The main aim is to make sure that everything you do is neat and securely fixed. You will need some simple equipment (see below) and a place to work with good light and a large counter surface, as well as a dry and cool place to store the flowers themselves.

Among the simple techniques covered in this section are simple wiring and using a glue gun, which I find a very useful piece of equipment.

Some other techniques – steaming open flowers and leaves, for example – have already been dealt with in the instructions for specific projects, and you will find these listed in the index on page 126.

Equipment

Shown below is the basic equipment you will find useful for your dried flower arrangements, and which you will need to tackle the projects in this book.

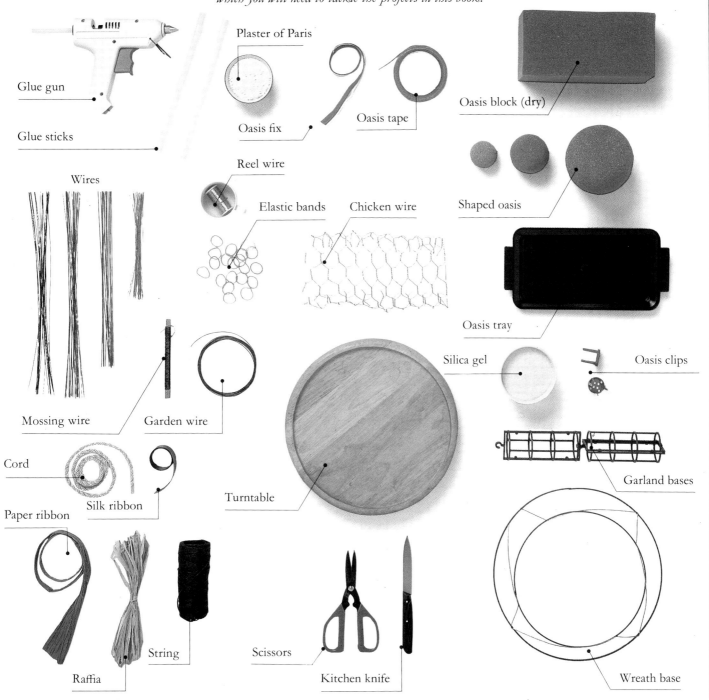

Glue gun

Glue sticks

Plaster of Paris

Oasis fix

Oasis tape

Oasis block (dry)

Reel wire

Wires

Elastic bands

Chicken wire

Shaped oasis

Oasis tray

Mossing wire

Garden wire

Silica gel

Oasis clips

Cord

Paper ribbon

Silk ribbon

Turntable

Garland bases

Raffia

String

Scissors

Kitchen knife

Wreath base

Bases

Whatever form of arrangement you have chosen, you will almost certainly require some kind of base for it, usually a container filled with florist's dry foam oasis. Oasis is a dry, spongelike material that holds the flower stems firmly in place. (Green foam oasis absorbs water for fresh flowers.) Oasis can be cut very easily to fit any shape, using a good, sharp kitchen knife. However, it breaks up fairly easily if you try to push large bunches of flower stems into it, so insert the flowers in small bunches or singly. Quite often, the oasis will need to be taller than the container so that you can insert flowers at right angles right down to the edge of the container. If any oasis is showing, it can be hidden with small pieces of moss.

For a stronger base – for a topiary tree, for example – I use plaster of Paris, which is readily available from hardware shops. It is very easy to use but dries hard very fast, so you cannot afford to waste time. You must make sure that you have all the ingredients on hand before you mix the plaster.

Other forms of base are created from hay or moss bound over a wire frame. Garlands need to have bases that will bend successfully to create loops; two forms of these are shown below.

1 Cut the oasis into neat rectangles approximately 3 in (8 cm) long by 1 in (2.5 cm) wide; cover with a rectangle of stiff netting and fasten the longer sides of the netting with staples.

3 Attach the flowers to the swag base in the usual way. The spaces between the sausages make it possible for the swag to be bent, as required.

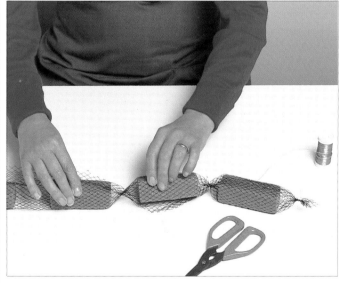

2 Twist small pieces of wire between each of the rectangles to fasten them together to create a string of "sausages" of oasis for the base.

4 The same effect can be achieved using ready-made plastic swag sausages. These are clipped together to form the required length for the whole swag.

Basket rims

If you wish to decorate the rim of a basket, you need a firm, solid base to which the flowers can be attached. Hay makes a good, inexpensive foundation provided it is secured tightly to the basket edge. You will need enough hay to make a thick rope about 2 in (5 cm) in diameter. Keep it in a plastic bag as you work with it and spread paper on the table, as hay tends to make a great deal of mess.

Making candle holders

Camellia leaves have been used for this candle holder, but ivy is an excellent alternative. Any large, shiny, evergreen leaf will do, provided it is reasonably pliable and the main stem is not too stiff. You can use this technique to decorate any straight-sided container. I normally glue the leaves into place using a glue gun (see page 120), then finish it by tying a raffia bow around it for decoration.

1 Pull the hay into a long rope shape. Attach it to the basket rim by pushing a wire through the basket underneath the hay rope and twisting the two ends together to hold it firmly in place.

1 Select an adequate number of similarly sized leaves in good condition. Heat up the glue gun, and then glue the leaves onto a glass tumbler, overlapping each leaf around the container with the leaf points just above the rim of the glass.

2 Repeat the wiring every few inches all the way around the basket rim, making sure you create an even, firm rope of hay.

2 Trim around the base of the glass with a pair of sharp scissors so that the leaves are level with the base of the glass.

3 Tidy up the completed hay rope by trimming off any surplus hay with a pair of scissors.

3 Spray the leaves with leaf shine spray, and tie a piece of raffia around the middle. Finish with a neat bow.

Using a glue gun

Glue guns come in either hot glue or low-temperature models. Either kind is suitable for dried flower arranging, but the advantage of a low-temperature gun is that there is less danger of being burned by the glue. They are generally reasonably priced and are useful for other jobs around the home. Glue guns help give your work a more professional appearance because you can place small dabs of glue exactly where you want them. Glue guns are easy to handle; many have their own stand. As the glue gun takes a few minutes to heat up, you will need to set it up and switch it on a little before it is actually needed.

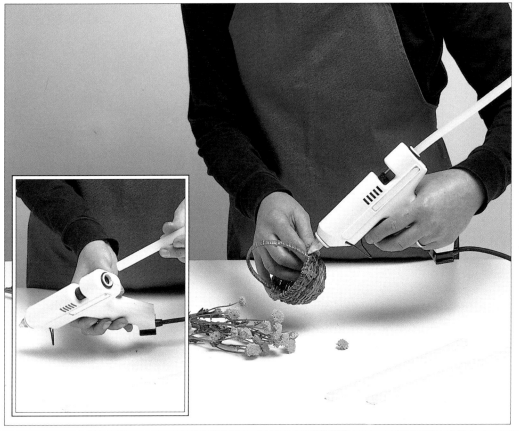

1 The gun uses sticks of solid glue inserted into the holder in the handle (see inset picture). The stick heats up when the gun is turned on. Press the trigger and melted glue comes out of the nozzle of the gun.

2 When using the glue gun, aim the nozzle at the exact part you wish to glue. When gluing flowers, make sure that you put the glue on the flower stems or the base of the flower head. If the petals are glued, they will simply fall away.

Wiring

Wire is the dried flower arranger's most useful tool; it comes in various thicknesses and lengths (see page 117). For very delicate stems use the finest rose wire, for most flowers use fine-gauge stub wire, and for heavy construction work use medium- or heavy-gauge stub wire. If you are creating an artificial stem with a tail of wire, you will need to use a medium-gauge wire. Bind delicate flowers into bunches with fine-gauge rose wire, then use a thicker gauge wire to create the tail.

If the wiring is likely to show, cover it with natural raffia. Think about how to hide the mechanics of the project as you make it. I normally arrange my bunches so that the heads of one bunch overlap the wired stems of another, successfully masking the wires.

Hard objects, including some nuts, seed heads, clay pots, and so on, can be wired successfully. This is a useful way of adding a contrasting texture to your dried flower arrangements. Walnuts have a small hole in the base which will take a wire, but other hard nuts, such as hazelnuts, brazil nuts, and pecan nuts, must be glued in place where required on the arrangement.

Fruit is very popular today as a variation in fresh flower arrangements. I use slices of grapefruit and oranges for decoration, dried in the oven, varnished, then wired together in fan shapes. Lemons and limes can also be prepared in this way, but the flesh is paler and less attractive. Fresh fruit can be used for decoration – particularly satsumas, kumquats, and oranges – but obviously no fresh fruit keeps very long so you may need to replace it from time to time. If you wire it with plastic-coated wire, rather than the normal metal wire, it will not rot so rapidly.

Throughout the book, I demonstrate how to wire various objects, but here are some useful techniques that you may want to use in any number of different arrangements.

Repairing broken flower heads

Roses are among the most expensive of dried flowers, but do not despair if you accidentally break off a head. Always keep any large flower heads that have lost their stems; if necessary they can all be wired to replace the missing stems. You will need to use medium-gauge stub wire for this purpose.

1 Push the wire through the flower head at its base until 2 in (5 cm) extends from the other side.

2 Bend both pieces of wire together, twisting the long end around the short one. Bend it downwards to create a stalk. Trim off any surplus wire.

Making a stem

You can make artificial stems for loose flower heads. Some flowers, such as helichrysum, are very brittle when dried, and it is best to make stems before drying.

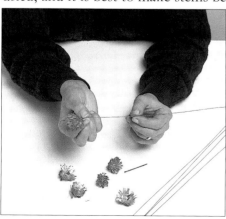

Make a hole in the base of the flower and push through a piece of medium-gauge stub wire. Bend the top of the wire to form a hook and pull it back down until it catches on the flower head.

Wiring a chestnut cluster

If you wish, first spray the nuts with polyurethane varnish to make them shiny. Then drive a nail through the nut to make a hole. Thread the nuts onto the wire and twist closed.

Wiring a cone

Place the wire 1 in (2.5 cm) up from the base of the cone, with about 3 in (8 cm) protruding across it. Push the wire into the scales of the cone so that it is hidden and twist the wire once around the cone. Twist the short end around the long one, and bend it downwards to make a tail.

Wiring a clay pot

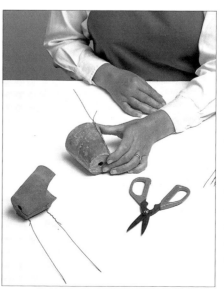

Insert one stub wire through the hole in the base of the pot and twist the ends together at the pot rim, leaving a long tail. Repeat with a second wire, but twist the ends together at the base of the pot, again leaving a long tail. These two tails can be used to attach the pot to the arrangement.

Wiring lotus seed heads

Lotus seed heads look hard and unyielding, but the back of the pod is hollow, and you can easily push a fairly stout wire through it.

Push the wire through at least 3 in (8 cm) of the pod. Bend both sides of wire together, twisting the longer piece around the shorter to form a stem, making sure it is tight enough to hold the pod firmly.

Wiring walnuts

Walnuts can be used singly or in a cluster, or sprayed and painted for decoration. They have a hole in the base into which you can push a medium-gauge stub wire.

Insert the wire into the hole in the base of the walnut. If it does not stay securely in the hole, remove the wire and dab a little glue on the end. Allow to dry.

Wiring fresh fruit

1 Select the side of the fruit that you want to have on display, and then thread medium-gauge stub wire right through the centre of the fruit.

2 Pull the wires together at the back of the fruit and twist together to make a stem.

Drying and wiring fruit slices

1 Slice the fruit fairly thinly, and put the slices onto a baking tray. Bake them in a very low oven, turning occasionally, until the fruit is dry. Allow it to cool. Spray the slices on one side with gloss varnish and allow to dry. Repeat with the other side.

2 When the fruit slices are dry, use medium-gauge stub wire to wire three or four slices together in a fan shape. They will keep for months once they have been sprayed.

Potpourri

I occasionally use potpourri in the centre of my arrangements of dried flowers, as in the Decorated Basket on page 91. You can make potpourri with all sorts of flowers, and leaves; experiment with different combinations until you find one you like.

To make it, mix all the flowers together with orris root powder in a large bowl. Add a few drops of essential flower oil and store in a roomy brown paper bag for a couple of weeks, to cure, turning it occasionally.

Below are two recipes I commonly use:

GARDEN FLOWER POTPOURRI

2 oz (50 g) pink rosebuds
2 oz (50 g) peony petals
2 oz (50 g) hibiscus petals
5 oz (125 g) lemon verbena petals
3 oz (75 g) lavender flowers
2 oz (50 g) chamomile flowers
1 oz (25 g) powdered orris root
A few drops rose geranium oil, or similar

SPICY POTPOURRI

4 oz (100 g) cut, dried orange peel
2 oz (50 g) bay leaves
3 oz (75 g) chamomile flowers
3 oz (75 g) lemon verbena flowers
2 oz (50 g) marigold flowers
2 oz (50 g) lemon grass
1 oz (25 g) powdered orris root
A few drops of lemon or lemon verbena oil

Making starched fabric bows

Starched fabric bows, sprayed in different colours, look very elegant, but are easy – and very cheap – to make. You will need plain white, cotton fabric – inexpensive, sheeting will do – white flour and laundry starch. For each bow, cut the fabric into a long strip roughly 36 in × 3 in (90 cm × 8 cm), and tie a bow in the fabric. Make up the starch paste using 2–3 heaped tablespoons of plain white flour and 1 tablespoon of laundry starch; stir in enough water to make a smooth paste the consistency of cream. Then follow the steps below. Once the bow is dry, you can spray it gold, silver, or whatever colour you wish (Turn an old cardboard grocery box or something similar on its side and use it as a shield for the spray.)

1 Using a spoon, dip the bow in the paste. Squeeze out any excess paste mixture from the bow, put it on a baking tray, and arrange the bow into the required shape.

2 Open out the tails of the bow and ruche them attractively. Bake in a warm oven until partly dry, usually about 8 minutes.

3 Adjust the bow to make the shape perfect, wire the knot so that you can attach the bow easily to your arrangement, and let it dry naturally. Then spray it whatever colour you wish.

Making a four-looped bow

Four-looped bows make an attractive finish for many arrangements, but it does take time and patience to make them look really professional. The proportions of the loops of the bow and the length of the tail are important. I like to keep the tails about $1\frac{1}{2}$ times the length of the loops of the bow. When you have tied the bow, finish off the ribbon tails by snipping them diagonally. To create a four-looped bow, cut a section of ribbon long enough for the purpose: decide how long you want the loops to be and allow roughly 4 times this length (to make the four loops of the bow), plus about 3 times the same length to make the knot and the tail.

1 Leave a length of ribbon for one end. Hold the ribbon between your thumb and forefinger and begin to make a figure eight.

4 Make the fourth loop, allowing the back of the loop and the tail of the ribbon to fall behind the bow.

2 Complete the other half of the figure eight, keeping the first loop firm with your other hand.

5 Holding the loops in place with one hand, bind the centre of the four loops together with a small piece of wire.

3 Start to make a third loop on top of the first two. Hold it firmly at the pivot point with your finger and thumb.

6 Cover the wire with another small piece of ribbon. Glue in place to make the knot in the centre of the bow.

SUPPLIERS

UK
Alan Barrett
Tudor Rose
11 Litchfield Avenue
Morden
Surrey SM4 5QS

Tel: 081 648 0747

Broadway Florist
155 Heath Road
Twickenham
Middlesex TW1 4BH

Tel: 081 892 5774

The Conran Shop
Garden Department
Michelin House
81 Fulham Road
London SW3 6RD

Tel: 071 589 7401

The Conservatory Flower Shop
13 Brewers Lane
Richmond
Surrey TW9 1HH

Tel: 081 940 2265

Country Choice
2 Blenheim Road
Minehead
Somerset TA24 5PY

Tel: 0643 706584

Clouds of Swansea
Unit 8
St Davids Centre
Swansea SA1 3LG

Tel: 0792 648093

Elmtree Dried Flowers
Elmtree Farm
Frocester Stonehouse
Gloucester

Tel: 0453 823274

Flowers by Arrangement
Downs House
Higher Downs
Altrincham
Cheshire WA14 2QL

Tel: 061 926 9404

The Flower Market
New Covent Garden
London SW8 5NF

Goldherb
Unit 7
Kestrel Close
Bridgend Industrial Estate
Mid Glamorgan CP31 3RW

Tel: 0656 669099

The Hop Shop
Castle Farm
Shoreham
Sevenoaks
Kent TN14 7UB

Tel: 0959 523219

Jenners
48 Princes Street
Edinburgh
EH2 2YJ

Tel: 031 225 2442

Lavenders of London
Unit 12
The Metro Centre
St Johns Road
Isleworth
Middlesex

Tel: 081 568 5733

Jenny Raworth
7 St Georges Road
St Margarets
Twickenham
Middlesex TW1 1QS

Tel: 081 892 3713

V V Rouleaux
201 New Kings Road
London SW6 4SR

Tel: 071 371 5929

Index

Authors' Acknowledgements

We would like to thank the following people who helped in creating this book and who above all made it a stimulating and enjoyable process:
Mike Newton, assisted by Peter Wragg, for his excellent and meticulous photography; Carol McCleeve for designing the book with patience and flair; Art Director Roger Bristow, Production Manager Kate MacPhee, and Publicity Manager Lisa Goldsmith at Collins & Brown; Ann Poe, Michele Italiano-Perla, and James Wagenvoord at Reader's Digest Association, New York. Special thanks go to Sarah Hoggett who edited the book. We would also like to thank Peter Rayner, Malcolm Hillier, Barry Graham and Pru Moray who provided some of the flowers and Peter Green from the Herbarium at The Royal Botanic Gardens, Kew, who helped in checking plant names.

Note: We would also like to stress that although every effort has been made to give correct quantities of ingredients for the projects, dried flower arranging is not an exact science, and amounts may vary depending on how tightly the flowers are packed.